THE
SUNSHINE
SKYWAY BRIDGE

D1224646

THE
SUNSHINE
SKYWAY BRIDGE
SPANNING TAMPA BAY

NEVIN D. SITLER & RICHARD N. SITLER

THE
History
PRESS

Published by The History Press
Charleston, SC 29403
www.historypress.net

Copyright © 2013 by Nevin D. Sitler and Richard N. Sitler
All rights reserved

All photographs taken from the archives of the St. Petersburg Museum of History and the authors' personal collections unless otherwise noted.

First published 2013

Manufactured in the United States

ISBN 978.1.62619.002.3

Library of Congress CIP data applied for.

Notice: The information in this book is true and complete to the best of our knowledge. It is offered without guarantee on the part of the authors or The History Press. The authors and The History Press disclaim all liability in connection with the use of this book.

All rights reserved. No part of this book may be reproduced or transmitted in any form whatsoever without prior written permission from the publisher except in the case of brief quotations embodied in critical articles and reviews.

To the Hough Family Foundation and Dr. Gary R. Mormino for their love of history, passion for the cultural arts and friendship—life's true bridge builders.

A special thank you to Veronica and Amanda.

CONTENTS

ACKNOWLEDGEMENTS

This story of linking the opposite shorelines of Tampa Bay with St. Petersburg and the rest of Florida's west coast—first by boat and then by bridge—would not have been possible without the generous open access to the archives of the St. Petersburg Museum of History. As the city's oldest museum and Florida's third-oldest historical museum, the St. Petersburg Museum of History has been collecting, preserving and communicating the rich and varied history of the area since 1922 (www.spmoh.org).

In addition, the *Tampa Bay Times* (formerly the *St. Petersburg Times*) provided enthusiastic support for the project from its archives. As a point of historical clarification, all of its photographs used in this book are credited to the original newspaper identity.

The authors are also grateful to Robert Neff of Fifth World Art for the use of several of his images. A longtime St. Petersburg resident, Robert has developed a widespread following for his photography and contemporary art. He has organized large-scale social media events for the Dali Museum, the St. Petersburg Honda Grand Prix and the World's Richest Tarpon Tournament in Boca Grande, Florida. More of his images may be viewed online at www.FifthWorldArt.com.

The degree of interest in our community—its past, present and future—that is shared by both of the following institutions is remarkable. Their assistance in this book has been invaluable and gratefully appreciated. The authors look forward to future projects and continued collaboration with these most instrumental organizations:

St. Petersburg Preservation Society

Since 1977, the St. Petersburg Preservation Society has been educating the public about local historic architectural resources. This organization works diligently toward the preservation, rehabilitation, restoration and/or acquisition of local natural, scenic and historical sites and structures (www.stpetepreservation.org).

Florida Studies Program (University of South Florida–St. Petersburg)

This graduate studies program brings together renowned faculty from history, English, geography, political science, anthropology and other disciplines to create an integrated, in-depth exploration of our state's changing identity and how Florida fits into matters of regional and global significance (www.usfsp.edu/coas/florida_studies/index.htm).

INTRODUCTION

There are more than 5,200 bridges throughout Florida that must be inspected and maintained on a regular basis by the Florida Department of Transportation. These structures span an assortment of keys, estuaries, canals, inland waterways, lakes and rivers. Some are movable; most are stationary. Some have official names; others have nicknames. And each has a six-digit state inventory number. But the icon of the state, the span that is today recognized by residents and tourists alike, is the Sunshine Skyway Bridge, located at the southern end of Pinellas County.

However, this award-winning cable-supported bridge is not the first structure to bear the Skyway name. Three generations of this bridge have crossed lower Tampa Bay, and each span boasts its own story. Before these steel-and-concrete engineering marvels completed a north–south connection, a determined soft-spoken man named George Gandy conquered the bay. Before him, of course, were the sailing ships of Spanish explorers and the dugout canoes of several Native American tribes. But those voyages and often-treacherous journeys did not provide regular or easy travel routes for the masses.

At the turn of the twentieth century, St. Petersburg was a quiet fishing village. The geographic isolation of the Pinellas Peninsula was exactly what attracted some of the early residents. Fishing was good, property was cheap, the pace was slow and the days were warm and sunny. But the need to communicate with and commute to Tampa became apparent. By 1909, a horse-and-buggy or Model-T trip around the bay was a daylong affair—longer if tires went flat or the rut-filled paths generously called "roads" became impassable.

A caravan of convertibles makes the ceremonial first crossing of the original Sunshine Skyway Bridge, opened to the public on Labor Day 1954. *Courtesy of* St. Petersburg Times.

Steamships like the *Caloosa* and the *Favorite* were popular and provided a relatively reliable means of transportation. But a cruise across the bay still meant two hours or more travel time and limited schedules. An east–west bridge was obviously needed. It would prove to be a formidable and expensive feat that would be viewed by skeptics as simply another Florida get-rich-quick scheme. In fact, when George Gandy enlisted the aid of Eugene M. Elliott to sign up investors and raise the necessary capital, even Elliott thought the bridge was a scam. During one of their financial meetings, Gandy expressed pleasure with the progress Elliott and his army of high-pressure salesmen had made, selling nearly $2 million worth of preferred Gandy stock in less than four months. When "Dad" Gandy proclaimed he was moving ahead with soil testing and dredging, an astonished Elliott asked, "You mean you're actually going to build this thing?"

It's worth noting that in 1914, aviator Tony Jannus flew his first paying passenger across Tampa Bay—ten years before anyone drove an automobile across a bridge. That twenty-three-minute flight is recognized as the historic start of scheduled airline service. But in those early days, a flight to Tampa was more for novelty purposes than actual business or vacation travel. But there were exceptions. At various times during the Benoist airboat's initial three-month operation, small bundles of unofficial "airmail" were carried as cargo. On the second day of flight operations from the yacht basin, the *St. Petersburg Times* seized a marketing opportunity and became the first newspaper in the country to be delivered by airplane. In the North, by 1926, Henry Ford had won the first federal airmail contract, and for a brief time, St. Petersburg airmail was driven across Gandy Bridge to the Tampa airport and flown to its destination. In 1929, with great fanfare, an official U.S. postal airmail service was permanently initiated in St. Petersburg, complete with a rooftop hand-off to a blimp of a package of airmail letters.

Whether by freighter, ferry, "Tin Lizzie" or seaplane, getting from one side of Tampa Bay to the opposite shore was still a major undertaking. But in 1924, industrialist George Gandy finally completed the vital east–west bridge connecting St. Petersburg to Tampa. However, the challenge of a north–south connection would remain unmet for the next three decades.

In 2010, more than fifty thousand vehicles crossed the Sunshine Skyway Bridge each day. But how many of these commuters recall having to drive around Tampa Bay to the north prior to bridges? How many paid three dollars to be ferried across the bay? And how many remember the construction of three different bridges called Sunshine Skyway from the 1950s to 1987? *The Sunshine Skyway Bridge* intends to tell those tales, tragedies and more. From the 1926 launch of the Bee Line Ferry to the design and construction of one of the world's longest cable-stayed bridges in 1987, the story of connecting the opposite shores of Tampa Bay as a collective work has remained unpublished until now.

For the past century, inventors and investors have sought creative methods of connecting an isolated peninsular Pinellas with the rest of Florida's west coast. From ferries to freeways, it has not been an easy task; lives were lost and fortunes spent.

Utilizing the St. Petersburg Museum of History's archival collection of nearly thirty thousand items, as well as those of colleagues, local universities and preservation societies, the images found in this publication are alluring and nostalgic. From construction, completion, disaster and demolition, these photographs highlight significant moments in the story of the bridges known as Davis Causeway, Courtney Campbell Causeway, W. Howard Frankland Bridge, Gandy Bridge, Friendship Trail Pedestrian Bridge, Sunshine Skyway and the Bee Line Ferry routes.

Additionally, a brief discussion of some of the smaller structures in the Greater Tampa Bay region is presented herein. Though these structures may not cross the open waters of the bay itself, they had and still have today an important impact on the entire geographic region by providing access to a host of both natural and man-made keys and isles. The various frenzies to sell, resell and sell again some of these instant tracts of waterfront properties attracted both permanent residents and the all-important tourist dollar.

Although the authors have researched and written this book as a serious and legitimate record of Tampa Bay's successful crossing, it is intended to be fun as well. Seriously, history doesn't have to be *all* that serious. At the end of each chapter, we've added a PS…no, not a postscript, a "post-span"—a few paragraphs about a unique individual, place or event that is somehow connected to that chapter's featured bridge. It is our hope that these post-span follow-ups may illustrate how the men who built our bridges did more than simply dredge sand, pour concrete and connect shorelines.

FIRST TO CROSS

1924

On the west coast of Florida, about halfway down the state, a dogleg northeastward channel cuts upward into the land. It reveals a seven-mile-wide entrance that allows the salt-laced Gulf of Mexico to pour into the inlet and splash on the shores. This estuary is Tampa Bay. At its entrance on the northern border sits peninsular Pinellas County. Manatee County, home of shoreline citrus farms and the sleepy town of Piney Point, borders the southern edge of the bay.

By the turn of the twentieth century, railroads were king. Rail cars packed with cash crops like lumber, phosphate and citrus from the South rolled north along these tracks, only to return with a different kind of cash crop—wealthy northern folk searching for a winter escape. Those who could not afford the hefty rail fees made the journey via horse and buggy along primitive trails. Most returned north enamored with the subtropical weather and sandy shores.

The Orange Belt Railroad brought both goods and northern visitors to the Pinellas Peninsula in June 1888 but was not a regular daily form of transport between Tampa and St. Petersburg. In fact, when the narrow-gauged locomotive known as Mattie first huffed and puffed its way into the village of roughly three hundred citizens, there was only one passenger aboard—a surely disappointed shoe salesman.

While their fondness for the area continued, visitors eagerly accepted improvements to their mode of travel. Henry Ford's 1908 introduction of the Model T sparked a new American revolution. His affordable, mass-produced automobile offered the mobility and freedom that neither

The Orange Belt Railroad locomotive Mattie was the first to enter Pinellas County in 1888.

Automobile caravans became a popular method of lobbying for better roads in Florida and other Atlantic Coast states.

trains nor horse and buggy could. Soon, communities like St. Petersburg experienced a yearly invasion of these "average citizens" descending on the town in horseless carriages.

Walter P. Fuller, in his *St. Petersburg and Its People*, wrote that in 1907, Dr. and Mrs. A.B. Davis were the first "daring adventurers" to drive by automobile from Tampa to St. Petersburg—a trip that took three and a half days. But the distinction of owning the town's first automobile goes to Edwin Tomlinson, the man who built St. Petersburg's famous Open Air Post Office. His 1905 Orient Buckboard, a one-cylinder, four-horsepower wonder, got stuck in practically every rut and mud hole along Central Avenue, but it was a harbinger of what was parked just around the proverbial corner. By 1908, the invasion of horseless carriages into St. Petersburg and other Florida communities became routine. Soon, rallies and caravans were organized throughout the state to lobby for support of improved roadways.

The new Florida explorers traveled hundreds of weather-beaten miles intending to stave off the cold of the North with balmy winds from the Gulf of Mexico and Tampa Bay. Many of these tourists became seasonal inhabitants, while others became full-time residents and lifelong boosters of the area.

The temporary World War I economic lull in tourism gave way to the early 1920s boom felt in many Florida cities. The postwar influx of permanent residents in St. Petersburg coupled with the seasonal invasion of tightfisted "Tin Can Tourists" led to intense land acquisitions and real estate dealings.

What started out as fields of tents, shanties and lean-tos packed with money-conscious visitors soon blossomed into residential housing and retail stores. New citizens built mail-order homes, and businesses flourished. With an average of twelve new citizens a day, 1920s St. Petersburg watched as old-fashioned agrarian transportation made way for the advanced technology of streetcars and the automobile.

Across the state—especially along the east coast—wealthy entrepreneurs like Carl Fisher emphasized the need for better roads, encouraging both public and private development. His eagerness to connect Point A with Point B via smoother, paved surfaces was a mantra repeated and promoted by Henry Ford, Harvey Firestone and Henry Flagler. Their motives were not altogether altruistic. After all, better roads meant better car sales, more tire production and travelers filling hotel rooms—three enterprises pioneered by these men.

Soon the demand for more suitable roads reaching farther into the isolated Pinellas Peninsula arose. The need to span Tampa Bay became an issue. New state roads were paved, including one linking Tampa to Miami.

At the prodding of the local women's beautification organization, city fathers acted fairly quickly to improve the rutted streets of St. Petersburg. As early as 1914, contractors began bidding on municipal paving projects that would continue for nearly twenty years. The end result was more than three hundred miles of St. Petersburg streets and alleys lined with granite curbs and surfaced with millions of nine-pound bricks. These pavers, as they were known, came from factories across the Southeast. A walk or bike ride down many of St. Petersburg's streets and alleys reveals the names of manufacturers like Southern Brick, Diamond, Rockmart and the ubiquitous Augusta Block. In addition to choosing the climate and the relaxed way of life, visitors frequently commented in chamber of commerce surveys that they enjoyed the beauty and comfort of the town's "wide brick streets."

Not wanting to lose potential tourist dollars to Hillsborough County and, especially, Tampa, St. Petersburg boosters pushed for bridging Tampa Bay in order to connect Pinellas with the new multi-lane highways "over there." Enter George Shepard Gandy.

Known by many as "Dad," the bespectacled George S. Gandy was a stern-looking fellow with a no-nonsense reputation that bordered on just plain stubborn. He'd been instrumental in the building of several profitable

George S. Gandy Sr.

trolley lines in and around Philadelphia before moving to Florida in 1902 at the request of F.A. Davis to serve as president of the St. Petersburg & Gulf Electric Railway Company. Gandy worked with various Davis companies, also serving for a time as president of the St. Petersburg Electric Light & Power Company. Disenchanted with Davis's financial methods, Gandy ultimately resigned these positions and struck out on his own. At the corner of Central Avenue and Fifth Street, Gandy built the La Plaza Theatre and office building. Some considered it to be the finest in Florida, but others spurned it as an outlandish "white elephant." Nevertheless, the structures were profitable ventures.

Ultimately, Gandy's transportation experience was the basis for his most memorable achievement. He viewed with disgust the fifty-two-mile-long route that connected St. Petersburg to Tampa. If Tampa Bay could be spanned, he reasoned, the cities could be made next-door neighbors, and both would profit. But even an optimist like Gandy realized that 1903 was not the time for the construction of a bridge. The Tampa Bay region simply had not developed enough to make it a profitable proposition. He resolved, however, that unless someone got ahead of him, "I'll build it myself."

With help from a man named Eugene M. Elliott, Gandy raised enough money at $42.50 per "investment unit" to make his dream a reality. Elliott reportedly thought the bridge was a scam, and during one of their financial meetings, he exclaimed, "You're actually going to build that thing?" Nevertheless, Elliott and his army of high-pressure salesmen sold nearly $2 million worth of preferred Gandy stock in less than four months. Gandy never invested a dime of his own money. By 1915, Gandy had plotted what he believed to be the best route and had obtained the needed right of ways from Hillsborough and Pinellas Counties. Al Gandy was secretary and treasurer of Ganbridge, Dad's aptly named bridge-building company that was literally cut out of the woods and built on the eastern shore of Tampa Bay. Al supervised all operations during the final year of the construction project, which throughout its duration would put more than 1,500 men to work.

Al's older brother, George S. Gandy Jr., better known as "Gidge," served on the company board of directors. Later, he would be involved in another sort of bridge-building effort, developing relations with Cuba and organizing the famed St. Petersburg–Havana Yacht Race.

Eugene Elliott's future was not nearly as positive. He used the sales force he had built to hustle properties across the central section of the state but continued to concentrate on the Tampa Bay area. He and his second wife lived in the upscale Coffee Pot Bayou area and apparently built something of a neighborhood reputation for heated arguments. On one particular afternoon, the household cook found Mrs. Elliott in the backyard lying unconscious at the bottom of the porch steps. Eugene rushed his wife to the hospital, but she did not survive. He was arrested and indicted, but the homicide charges were finally dropped, leaving Elliott to drift in and out of St. Petersburg for several years, dying penniless.

At the turn of the nineteenth century, the passenger steamer *Favorite* lived up to its name as a chosen method of commuting between the two major towns that shared the Tampa Bay shoreline. The nearly two-hour crossing was one dollar per round trip. At the height of tourist season, as many as five trips per day were scheduled. But this method of travel between St. Petersburg and Tampa would soon prove inadequate. Passenger boat service could get one across the bay, but visitors and residents wanted their automobiles too.

The steamer *Caloosa*, originally owned and operated by the Atlantic Coast Railroad, was sold to the Independent Steamship Company in 1903. It provided passenger service between St. Petersburg and Sarasota. The steamers *H.B. Plant* and *Manatee* were soon added to the fleet, with each ship completing the two-hour run twice daily.

In 1914, ten years before anyone drove across Tampa Bay, aviator Tony Jannus flew his first paying passenger from the St. Petersburg yacht basin to Tampa's waterfront.

This Benoist (pronounced *ben-wah*) airboat, flown by Tony Jannus on the world's first regularly scheduled passenger flight, was powered by a seventy-five-horsepower Roberts engine. Years later, a company banner attached to one of the wings would be carried into space on a NASA mission.

With a winning auction bid of $400, former mayor Abram C. Pheil paid his way into history books. That twenty-three-minute flight on New Year's Day is recognized as the official start of the world's first scheduled airline service. It's true, the flight could have been a little quicker, but Jannus was forced to set the airboat down in Tampa Bay to make adjustments to the propeller drive chain. Passenger Pheil didn't even get a discount for serving as a mechanic's assistant on that inaugural flight repair stop. After landing on the Hillsborough River before an estimated crowd of nearly two thousand Tampa spectators, the former mayor had a strange but simple request. "Will someone please unbutton my coat?" he asked, displaying a pair of still-greasy hands. For the next three months, Jannus operated the flight service, sometimes skimming just feet over the water and occasionally making other landings in the bay to make engine or other critical adjustments. During its relatively short tenure, regularly scheduled flights transported passengers, mail and even daily issues of the *St. Petersburg Times*.

The original contract was for ninety days but continued for a few weeks beyond that before Jannus moved on to other aviation career opportunities. However, like steamships, air travel across the bay couldn't handle the volume of would-be commuters. Gandy's bridge was still sorely needed. Incidentally, Abe Pheil's wife did not share his enthusiasm for flying and, for a time, was unaware of his extravagant expense. She waited twenty-five years before taking her first airplane ride as part of an anniversary flight in celebration of her late husband's historic ride.

Even the beginning of the airline was historic. On December 17, 1913, exactly ten years to the day after Orville and Wilbur Wright made their first flight at Kitty Hawk, the St. Petersburg–Tampa Airboat Line signed a contract with the City of St. Petersburg to provide two passenger flights per day, six days a week for a three-month period. Regular service was to begin on January 1, 1914. The agreement stipulated that for each day the scheduled flights were made on time, the city would pay forty dollars a day for the first month. The rate would then drop to twenty-five dollars per day during February and March. Now a century later, complaints about baggage charges by some airlines prove to be nothing new. Airboat passenger limits were set at two hundred pounds gross weight, including hand baggage. Extra weight was charged at five dollars per one hundred pounds. Tony Jannus made a total of nine flights that historic opening day, earning the company more than $600, which was donated to the city to purchase harbor lights. During this ninety-day period, 1,205 passengers were safely flown on regularly scheduled flights over and around the bay.

Ironically, one of his early paying passengers was "Gidge" Gandy, the bridge builder's eldest son.

The airline operated five weeks beyond the original three-month contract, but passenger numbers began to dwindle, and both Tony and his older brother Roger, also a pilot, wanted to pursue other aviation goals. On April 27, Roger piloted the last Jannus flight over Tampa Bay. The world's first airline had laid the groundwork for what would become a worldwide multibillion-dollar industry.

By 1917, others had caught on to Gandy's idea of bridging the bay. The Tampa Atlantic & Gulf Railroad Company filed plans to build its bridge, but the competition didn't deter Gandy. He rallied civic support and petitioned the War Department's board of engineers for approval of his plan above all others. Developer Walter P. Fuller and his son H. Walter Fuller became believers in the Gandy dream, throwing in their support and some of their cash. In his book *St. Petersburg and Its People*, Walter P. Fuller goes so far as to all but take full credit for the idea of building a bridge to Tampa, noting that he discussed it on more than one occasion with Dad Gandy. The Fullers correctly predicted that a bridge would make their land investments very profitable.

Even though Gandy won the support of leading public officials like U.S. senator Duncan Fletcher and Congressman Herbert Drane, as well as backing from major area banks, War Department engineers were skeptical. They initially withheld their approval because to them it looked as if the same person had written all the glowing endorsements of the bridge's proposal.

Erupting like Jack Nicholson in his classic line from *A Few Good Men* ("You can't handle the truth!"), Gandy lacerated board members. "They bear the stamp of one man, you say?" he uncharacteristically shouted. "You bet they do! And I'm that man! If that bridge is ever built...it will be by some fellow who gets behind it like I have and never quits." The engineers were impressed and gave their immediate approval.

The grant was made on February 11, 1918, about ten months after the United States entered World War I. It became nearly impossible to secure construction materials. Gandy's engineers took advantage of the delay by making new surveys and selecting a natural rock shelf that allowed a deeper, twenty-three-foot channel across the middle of the bay. But the high price of construction materials following the war added to the delay. Gandy's plan called for trolley tracks down the very center, and gutter-like depressions can be seen in many construction photos. But steel rails were never laid, and no trolley ever crossed the span.

Following the Great War, a local interest in civilian flying once again emerged with hometown-bred James Albert Whitted, a freshly discharged naval aviator, setting up flying services at St. Petersburg's Spa Beach. Whitted had competition from a Tennessee barnstormer named Johnny Green, who actually took over operation of the Jannus-originated airboat line after Tony and Roger moved on to other ventures. Like Whitted, Green enlisted as a navy flight instructor, but he had crashed in Key West and spent his war years as a signal corps inspector. Both pilots shuttled hundreds of passengers across the waters of Tampa Bay. Rumor had it that Johnny Green was far more profitable than Whitted, due in part to the fact that he ran a local watering hole called the Green Lantern adjacent to his hangar. Plus, there were suspicions that he had a lucrative side business of running contraband to Cuba. But this was not destined to be the final method of spanning the bay.

Longtime city publicity director John Lodwick built an impressive list of accomplishments during his career promoting the Sunshine City. But the albatross around his neck happened to be a blimp. Lodwick and some former

Many residents felt that Albert Whitted, the model of a handsome, dashing pilot, was destined to become a movie star. Here he poses with his airboat, the *Blue Bird*, and a bevy of Max Sennett's bathing beauties.

Goodyear associates in Akron, Ohio, were overly optimistic in predicting that more than 150,000 tourists would fill Florida skies in search of rest and relaxation. That number was never realized. Certainly, the baby zeppelins were great attention-grabbers for special events such as the initiation of local airmail service, sporting venues and beer promotion. But for regular commuter travel across Tampa Bay, it would be bridges, not blimps.

Finally, in 1922, mule-drawn carts and plain old brute strength got George Gandy's engineering marvel off the ground as work started on both shores. Twenty years after his plan was conceived and seven years after the first surveys were made, a serious financing schedule was unveiled. Nearly four thousand Florida residents and tourists invested in Gandy's dream, and several dozen more joined in after construction began.

On September 26, 1922, Gandy escorted the wife of former partner Walter P. Fuller to watch as the first sand was pumped for the long causeways. Two days earlier, the *Tuscawilla* had become the first dredge to work on the Pinellas causeway. A second dredge, the *Florida*, started a month later, and the third dredge, *Reliable*, began work on March 28, 1923. Continuous dredging operations took more than eighteen months,

After years of planning and waiting, work finally started on Gandy's bridge in 1922. The steamer, seen in the center background, was most likely used to transport workmen and supplies between shorelines.

moving approximately 2,500,000 cubic yards of sand from the bottom of Old Tampa Bay.

Before concrete pouring could begin, a construction camp was established "out in the wilderness." Bunkhouses, machine shops, dining halls and the proverbial company store had to be provided for a workforce of nearly 1,500 men. Appropriately named Ganbridge, the camp was a city unto itself during the spring and summer of 1923, with more than a dozen buildings and large material staging areas. The eastern shore of Old Tampa Bay was a place of noise and smoke, with a seemingly endless parade of cranes, locomotives, pile drivers, trucks, concrete mixers, tugboats, tractors and drilling outfits.

On May 15, 1923, whistles screeched, men cheered and guns were fired into the air as the first concrete was poured at the pile-casting plant. Nearly 2,400 reinforced concrete piles, some as long as sixty feet, would eventually be poured, cured and then steam-hammered into the bay floor.

"Hands Across the Bay" was the phrase used to promote the Sunshine Skyway Bridge, but that wouldn't be for another quarter century. A 1924 photo of company field supervisors shows the centerline section of the Gandy Bridge that was to accommodate trolley rails. Why the men chose

Gandy originally proposed a center lane that would provide trolley service. Electric streetlights ran the full length of the span, but no trolley rails or power lines were ever installed.

to hold hands is unclear, but their outstretched arms do provide a human yardstick to judge the nine-foot lane width of "the world's longest toll road."

By midyear, more than 100 laborers were living in Ganbridge. The construction camp even boasted its own water filtration system for making and pouring concrete. Several work gangs concentrated on preparing roadway approaches, while slightly higher-paid workers drove concrete pilings into the bedrock of the bay. In all, more than 1,500 workmen would temporarily call Ganbridge home.

The value of Gandy Bridge to Pinellas and Hillsborough Counties proved itself quickly. Great sections of land once considered almost worthless were opened up for development. Tracts of scrubland along the bridge route that once could be purchased for less than $25 an acre skyrocketed to $1,000 an acre. Much to the Fullers' delight, the better tracts pulled in many times that price. Property along Fourth Street, the main connection between downtown St. Petersburg and the bridge, jumped from $500 a lot to three times that amount. Surprisingly, Gandy did not share in the great profits made from the buying and selling of this adjoining land. His profits came from overseeing and operating the bridge.

With the possible exception of the W. Howard Frankland Bridge, St. Petersburg, as a collective civic group, has always taken "ownership" of Tampa Bay's remaining bridges. Even though each span connects opposing shorelines, the popular argument seems to be, "It's a St. Pete bridge." Tampa newspapers promoted George Gandy's accomplishment by snubbing St. Petersburg and emphasizing that they were "now connected to Largo." Thirty years later, personal and political feuds would keep one end of the Sunshine Skyway Bridge out of Hillsborough County, locating its terminus in Manatee County and the city of Bradenton.

Because Gandy lived and worked in the Sunshine City, it is natural to assume that once he had completed his dream, any form of dedication ceremony would certainly take place on the Pinellas County shoreline. And in truth, most of the picnicking, singing and family entertainment did take place in Williams Park and in the ballroom of the Huntington Hotel. But a ceremonial ribbon of flowers was cut at the Tampa entrance, allowing the entourage of visiting state governors, reporters and other dignitaries to proceed to the Pinellas shore.

The formal opening finally came on November 20 with a guest list that included the governors of seventeen states. A seventy-three-year-old George Gandy watched as the first of nearly ten thousand cars drove across his dream highway. Following the formal dedication, a motorcade of dignitaries

This is one of the few known remaining photographs of the official Gandy Bridge dedication with crowds gathered at water's edge.

gathered at the St. Petersburg Yacht Club to socialize. An evening celebration in Williams Park featured a concert with the debut performance of a fox trot entitled "Gandy Bridge" composed by Mrs. Flora Overly Wilson.

Before the completed span, travel from St. Petersburg to Bradenton required a ninety-mile adventure. Gandy's bridge connected Tampa to the gulf beaches and eliminated nearly half of the St. Petersburg–Bradenton journey, having an immediate effect on Tampa Bay–area residents and visitors alike. As with almost any innovation, there were those who had immediate objections to change, the most pronounced coming from automobile drivers who believed charging a toll was, literally, highway robbery. There was an attitude that once any sort of pavement was in place, it was a God-given right for motorists to use that route free of charge—a concept still grumbled by some as they toss coins into a toll plaza basket. But now, thanks to Gandy, the commute was a fraction of the time it once took to negotiate rutted trails around the bay, highlighted sometimes by an unplanned overnight journey.

The drawbridge did result in occasional traffic delays. In almost all cases, maritime traffic received priority over vehicular traffic, and one boat could stall bridge traffic for fifteen minutes or more—often long enough to get out of your car, visit with other travelers, pose for photos or surreptitiously throw a line in the water. (Gandy didn't charge an extra fee for that privilege.)

The bridge even provided an unexpected plus to area farmers. With proper advance notice, small herds of cattle, horses and pigs could cross the bay on foot for a toll of twenty cents a head. For the first two years, the toll to cross Gandy's bridge was seventy-five cents per car and driver plus ten cents per passenger. From 1926 to 1928, the fare dropped to fifty cents plus a nickel per passenger. By 1940, the basic fee was thirty-five cents. Folks in the passenger seats were still charged five cents a head, thank you.

Newspaper ads explained that for safety reasons, fishing and pedestrians were not allowed. In short order, Gandy would easily make money for his investors and himself. But soon, most civilian travel was curtailed or reduced

George Gandy never made any money from land investments related to the bridge. His wealth came from the tollbooth, which originally charged seventy-five cents per car and driver.

due to wartime fuel and tire rationing. All toll charges were suspended on April 27, 1944, as a "wartime necessity" declared by the War Department, which had taken over operation of the bridge.

Subsequent spans built along this same path would eliminate the drawbridge with higher spans. By 1991, after several modifications and upgrades, highway planners agreed that a new bridge parallel to the original 1920s span made the most sense. They concluded that not only was it the easiest and cheapest method, but it was also the most environmentally safe route. Both terminus points in Hillsborough and Pinellas Counties became popular fishing locations.

As improvements were made, the Gandy Bridge, for a brief time, would actually be three parallel Tampa Bay structures. County commissioners made deals, and a plan was crafted to convert the original structure into a recreational bridge for the benefit of bicyclists, tourists and fishermen. But dollars dictated, and once again, following a theme all too common in Florida, demolition was cheaper than preservation. The "longest toll bridge in the world" was blown up. Years later, the same demolition expert would detonate explosive charges that turned one of the Sunshine Skyway Bridges into reef-building rubble. The 1956 version of the bridge remains in place, but its future is on shaky ground—both literally and figuratively. Engineers have stated that the decaying structure, now known as the Friendship Trail Bridge and dedicated to pedestrian-only activities, should be demolished. Some preservationists want to modify and save the span. Time and money will ultimately decide how enduring friendship really is.

The novelty of an automobile ride was an exciting event for many. The Sunday family drive after church was a new and popular American pastime, and a drive across the water was just icing on the cake. But for some residents on both sides of the bay, another adventure was being threatened by this "progress." Passenger travel on a steamer as large as the *Favorite* wasn't just a boat ride—it was an event. Getting there was often as important and as much fun as the intended destination. The ship could carry as many as one thousand passengers, each paying two dollars for a round trip. Twice-daily cruises made commuting possible, but for most it was still not a daily ritual.

However, meeting these freighters at the dock was part of the daily routine for newspaperman Ralph Reed, a beat reporter at the *St. Petersburg Times*. At that time, William Straub managed the day-to-day operations, and Paul Poynter handled financial matters. They shared similar views on what a newspaper should and should not be, and both knew the value of folks reading about their friends, their neighbors and themselves. These were known as the

A ride on the steamship *Favorite* was more than a voyage—it was an adventure.

personals—one or two lines of gossip, good news, pithy thoughts or blatant bragging. Poynter wasn't happy unless each edition had at least forty or fifty such items. For Reed, the solution was simple: ask the travelers where they were going, where they had been and what they did. In one respect, his daily reports were the low-tech version of today's social network tweeting:

> *Mrs. H.T. Malcolm of Lansing, Mich. is visiting her daughter and son-in-law, Mr. and Mrs. Robert Wilson. She intends to stay the entire season.*

> *F.A. Davis yesterday reviewed electric plant expansion contracts with officials in Tampa.*

> *On board the Caloosa to a Tampa church meeting, Harold Adams caught an eighteen-pound red snapper. The Presbyterian ladies circle prepared his catch for lunch along with snap peas, corn and mincemeat pie.*

With more travelers moving about in their own vehicles, Ralph Reed's job as a journalist got a little tougher. He couldn't easily interview folks at the Gandy tollgate, but on occasion he chatted with and wrote about drivers and their passengers who were delayed by the open drawbridge. Reed continued

A postcard featuring the Bee Line Ferry *Pinellas*.

to ride on trolley cars and meet railroad depot passengers, asking the same questions for each day's personals posting. A brief visit with Bee Line Ferry passengers always seemed to provide enough fodder to keep bosses Poynter and Straub satisfied.

While George Gandy was accomplishing the east–west dream, St. Petersburg real estate pioneers J.G. Foley and Charles Carter devised a solution for the north–south problem. The partnership launched the Bee Line Ferry Company in February 1926. Crossings made by the *Fred D. Doty*, the line's first vessel, were an instant success. For minimal fees, passengers could park their autos onboard and leisurely watch seagulls and pelicans during their forty-five-minute ride across the bay. The *Doty* was soon replaced by a fleet of three diesel ferryboats: the *Pinellas*, *Manatee* and *Sarasota*.

The aptly named trio shuttled about 1,500 automobiles and their passengers daily, saving their clients forty-nine miles of non-air-conditioned driving each way. A round trip cost three dollars, and passengers without an automobile paid twenty-five cents each way. The astonishing increase in automobile traffic on Pinellas roads created a wait that often lasted for hours. Nevertheless, the ferry ride offered foodstuffs, as much salt air as one could breathe and a welcome respite from the bone-jarring drive around Tampa Bay.

Nineteen months after the Bee Line's maiden voyage, E.J. McMullen signed on as a ferryman. He had deep family roots in Pinellas County and was proud of that heritage. During his twenty-eight-year tenure, Captain

McMullen and his crew encouraged ferry passengers to ask questions regarding the various species encountered along the route. Crewmen knew "their Florida" and were eager to impress, befriending many riders over the next few decades. Whether they were preoccupied with a "hot poker game going on" or busy securing cargo, deckhand Huddy "Buck" LeVar recalled that crew members frequently "forgot" to collect the required quarter from local youths for the return trip to St. Petersburg. In 1934, Early McMullen joined his father's crew swabbing decks and laboring at other deckhand duties before finally earning a captain's license. But World War II temporarily split the father-and-son team. Since the Army Air Corps controlled the ferries during the war, the elder McMullen assisted his country by shuttling locals and soldiers from Tampa to MacDill Army Air Field. Trading cantankerous pelicans for kamikaze pilots, Early remained on a ship during the war. However, he went from piloting a one-hundred-ton vessel across Tampa Bay to serving as a sailor on a three-thousand-ton destroyer in the Pacific Ocean.

The ferry linked St. Petersburg to Bradenton and shortened the drive between those two cities by sixty miles. The Great Depression slowed operations slightly, but by the mid-1930s, traffic was bustling.

During World War II, massive military camps and remote installations filled Florida with over 2 million military trainees. St. Petersburg alone received more than 100,000 airmen, seamen and soldiers. The War Department took operational control of the Gandy Bridge and eliminated tolls because servicemen assigned to or rotating through nearby MacDill Field frequently traveled across the bridge. The navy took over operational control of the Bee Line Ferry.

With plenty of empty hotels, wide spaces and Pacific Island–like landscapes, the Sunshine City was a perfect housing and training ground for troops. The brick-clad streets of downtown St. Petersburg now served as parade routes for soldiers and airmen—not just for holiday celebrations but also for required drill and ceremony practice.

At nearby Bayboro Harbor, more than twenty-five thousand maritime service cadets trained and occupied housing that would eventually become part of the University of South Florida at St. Petersburg. Every major hotel in the city served as a military billet or teaching facility. However, chamber of commerce officials and municipal boosters staged a massive publicity campaign, sending press releases to newspapers across the country claiming the city could always handle a few more visitors. By counting tourist cabins, rental homes, campgrounds, trailer parks and small, off-the-beaten-path hotels, the tourism supporters claimed that more than 6,500 accommodations

The near-tropical conditions of remote Pinellas and other South Florida counties made ideal training grounds for thousands of soldiers, airmen and sailors during World War II.

were available and affordable. And visitors did come—many were relatives of servicemen who were stationed or training here. Some facilities continued as government accommodations even after the war, with the Don CeSar Hotel at Pass-A-Grille evolving into a Veterans' Affairs complex. At the conclusion of World War II, the Port Authority of St. Petersburg, with assistance from the former owners, purchased the ferries from the government and resumed normal operations. Years after the war, Dad Gandy petitioned the federal government for reimbursement of lost toll bridge income. He was awarded more than $2.3 million plus interest.

For some ferry commuters, the ride across Tampa Bay was a relaxing excursion and a connection with nature. For others, it was an adventure. And for still others, it was a necessity. But capacities were certainly limited; even a modest two-lane bridge was predicted to be capable of handling more vehicles in one hour than the Bee Line Ferry could accommodate in an entire day with the entire fleet operating on schedule. Weather permitting, ferries closely followed a daily thirty-minute departure schedule from 7:30 a.m. to 9:00 p.m.

The trip across the bay was promoted as more than just a way of getting from one side to the other. Brochures described the junket as a nature excursion that afforded commuters the opportunity to soak in the tranquil surroundings, worry-free. The one-way fare was increased to $1.75 per car, sometimes with as many as one hundred automobiles waiting in line. Operational costs included raises for boat captains, who now earned $1.15 per hour, while deck hands made $0.65. The ferry would sometimes make trips as late as 10:00 p.m. to accommodate dog track bettors at the Sarasota Kennel Club.

The Bee Line Ferry operated from the foot of Fourth Street South on Pinellas Point. Buses were charged based on length at ten cents per foot plus twenty-five cents for the first ten passengers—additional passengers and the driver were free. A Bee Line Ferry schedule card boasted a three-dollar round-trip fare, while many walk-on passengers traveled free of charge.

Following World War II, the McMullens were eager to resume their roles as captains of the Bee Line Ferry. Their joy, however, was short lived. A bridge opening the Pinellas County peninsula was desperately needed to accommodate the growing number of automobiles and passengers. Local voters responded by approving a $15 million bond issue to construct the bridge. The 1947 measure mandated that all repaid monies come from tolls collected, not from taxes raised. The ferry's days were numbered—the Sunshine Skyway Bridge was coming.

The Bee Line's southern terminus, Piney Point, was reached in about forty minutes and traversed, as the company promoted, "the last American Frontier."

Post-Span

Early J. McMullen
1921–2003

In 2002, forty-eight years after the Sunshine Skyway Bridge took away his Bee Line ferryman's job, seventy-two-year-old Early J. McMullen still looked the part of a sailor—but now in a floppy golf hat. He wrote to President Ronald Reagan requesting that ferry service across the bay be resumed. He admitted that he missed "those days," but his love for the open water had turned to a passion for music and mastery of the harmonica. McMullen told a reporter that his letter to Reagan included an audiotape of him playing what he called "cracker rock-and-roll, with fewer rocks." Early didn't get the ferry service back in operation, but he was invited to perform at the White House. He spent the last year of

Early J. McMullen. *Courtesy of* St. Petersburg Times.

his life playing tunes at his favorite coffee shop in Tampa and giving away free harmonicas. If you were interested and had the time, he'd even throw in a free lesson or two.

Chapter 2

BEACH-BOUND BRIDGES

1915–1938

George Gandy accomplished the over-water connection between Tampa and St. Petersburg in 1924 with the "world's longest toll bridge"; however, the impact of bridges in the Tampa Bay area would be incomplete without mentioning the barrier islands of Pinellas County. Few remember that the first bridge to the beaches was constructed nearly a decade prior to Gandy's world record–setting span to Tampa.

Constructed in 1915 at a cost of around $7,500, a four-hundred-foot-long toll bridge was erected from the mainland to Indian Rocks Beach. The fifteen-foot-wide structure, about a half mile south of present-day Walsingham Road, cost a whopping $0.15 to cross one way and a quarter for a round-trip excursion. The hand-operated swinging drawbridge proved to be a picturesque sight but was considered a terrible bottleneck for beach-bound traffic. By 1938, commuters demanded that Pinellas County commissioners take over the bridge and remove the toll. Two decades and $720,000 later, a replacement bridge spanned the gap just a few thousand feet north of the original structure. While Clearwater and Indian Rocks' beaches beckoned visitors, the southern islands off mainland St. Petersburg were coming into the twentieth century.

Before British Columbia and Pennsylvania license plates adorned nearly every other automobile that crossed the modern bridges onto St. Pete Beach, there existed a different island. It was a terrain devoid of ribbons of pavement and flashing neon lights tempting tourists to a round of tiki-themed miniature golf or promising patrons air conditioning and color televisions in every room. In their place, scrubby thickets, loamy hammocks and black mangroves dotted the wide bleached beaches and coastal sand dunes of Long Key.

One of several barrier islands skirting the western shores of Pinellas County, Long Key (not to be confused with the atoll that lies amongst the emerald string of coral-formed keys south of Miami) is the southernmost landmass forming central Florida's gulf beaches. Located at the mouth of Tampa Bay and running northward, Boca Ciega Bay separates the east coast of Long Key from the mainland and provides a reflective ravine for the rising sun. On the island's opposite shores, the Gulf of Mexico's mythic "green flash" signals the day's end for western witnesses. From gulf to bay, the island, always changing in size with the tides, is, at its southernmost point, barely a few hundred feet wide. Long Key's mass lies in its length, which is about seven miles.

By the time Prohibition had found its way to Long Key, the barrier islands were structurally connected to the mainland. Owning five hundred acres on the northern portion of Long Key, William J. McAdoo had hired a St. Petersburg's Municipal Pier contractor to erect a span across Boca Ciega Bay to connect the island to the mainland. Running two lanes from the west shore of St. Petersburg at Villa Grande Avenue, motorists on William McAdoo's bridge would exit at today's Eighty-seventh Avenue on Long Key. The rickety wood-slatted construction, toll and all, connected St. Petersburg

Loose, broken and missing boards were almost a trademark of McAdoo's Bridge, and that (or just poor driving) nearly sent this Dodge Brothers automobile into the drink.

to McAdoo's new project, St. Petersburg Beach. Despite complaints that McAdoo, according to Jari Mogavero, site coordinator of the Gulf Beaches Historical Museum in Pass-A-Grille, "charged a toll and operated at his whim," his bridge was a great achievement for local tourism and those bound for the barrier islands.

While the Pass-A-Grille bridge lasted nearly a decade, McAdoo's landholdings on Long Key were entrenched in legal issues and greed for many years. Regardless of his business prowess, McAdoo and his teeth-rattling bridge drew attention to St. Petersburg and helped establish its gulf beaches.

One entertaining tale of William McAdoo's attempt at selling his grand plan of a seaside attraction on the small island deals with boomtime antics and buried treasure. Another small barrier island, just to the north, bordered McAdoo's landholdings. With the help of a few accomplices and a sturdy wagon, McAdoo devised a devious plan to make headlines for his beach assets. In the stealth of night, he buried a large wooden chest loaded with lead weights near water's edge. The following morning, ensuring that several tourists were within view to witness the "discovery," McAdoo and his crew removed the "treasure," loading it onto a drawn wagon. With McAdoo driving and his shotgun-brandishing partners protecting their find, the trio headed into St. Petersburg, where the "treasure chest" took center stage in the front window of a local downtown bank.

The modern-day pirate's plan backfired, recalls local resident Frank Hurley Jr. An incorrect account soon spread that the chest had been unearthed on the island adjacent to McAdoo's St. Petersburg Beach, stripping his island of a tall tale and permanently labeling the key to the north as "Treasure Island." Although the Pinellas barrier islands have a long, rich history of settlers, "real development," wrote Karl Grismer in *The Story of St. Petersburg*, "began with the completion of the bridge." No longer required to secure passage aboard a vessel to visit infamous Pass-A-Grille, Sunday drivers and winter residents welcomed the span. They turned out in droves to visit pristine beaches, sup on fifty-cent seaside smorgasbords and gawk at Thomas Rowe's impressive Don CeSar Hotel.

McAdoo's bridge was severely damaged during the near legendary October 25, 1921 hurricane, which lashed the area with floods and high winds. Although Pass-A-Grille was rebuilt, it met its demise shortly after the toll-free Corey Avenue Causeway was constructed about a mile south.

Promoted by businessman and hotelier Thomas Rowe, the need for an improved roadway system connecting mainland St. Petersburg to Long Key became evident. By 1925, a bond for $1,250,000 was issued to accomplish this goal. Of course, Rowe wanted more visitors and guests to stay at his opulent Don CeSar resort, but state authorization was required for the bridge construction to begin. With the persistence and support of Pinellas County commissioner S. Jack Corey, the free causeway plan finally got the green light.

By May 1927, over two hundred men toiled on construction of the Pasadena–Long Key connection. Within five months, the span was completed. Designed with Grecian-style railings, the thirty-foot-wide causeway featured a sixty-foot-long draw span and joined land at the widest point of the island. Soon, thousands of weekend visitors would use the toll-free Boca Ciega Causeway. The 1925 referendum that Commissioner Corey fought for also called for the financing of a connection between Treasure Island and Madeira Beach. The end result, notes St. Pete Beach historian Roberta Whipple, was a "scenic motoring loop" from mainland Pinellas to the beaches and back.

An earlier hurricane, the "Great Gale of 1848," was reputedly responsible for the creation of a new geographic feature on the gulf shores: an inlet known as John's Pass. Actually, the storm just intensified the normal shifting of spoils and passes created by the wind and currents. John's Pass was named for a turtle fisherman named John Levick (also written Lavique) when he and his partner were returning home from selling a load of turtles in New Orleans. John was steering for an entrance called Blind Pass when he was surprised to discover that the storm had created a new opening into Boca Ciega Bay, separating Treasure Island and Maderia Beach. Since his turtling partner, Joe Silva, was asleep at the time, John claimed naming rights to the find.

Historian Fuller notes that the original pass may have been nearly a mile from where it is today thanks to the erosion and redepositing of beach sands. The first generation of a bridge linking the two tourist communities was built in the mid-'20s; a second version was completed in 1971. The most recent renovation to John's Pass Bridge increased its vertical clearance to one hundred feet, enabling more waterway traffic to pass through without opening the drawbridge and allowing about fifteen thousand vehicles to cross daily. Work was completed in 2011 at a final cost of $77 million.

Not all island-connecting bridges were headed to the gulf beaches, and for that matter, not all islands were actual islands. Turning liquid into land, as the adage goes, civic leaders and developers trenched and filled along the shorelines, creating artificial inlets and man-made islands for further

With movable bridges, the rule is that watercraft have the right of way. This frequently caused traffic delays of thirty minutes or more at St. John's Pass.

speculation and lot sales. Resident C. Perry Snell epitomized the term "land developer" through his dredged enclave, Snell Isle.

Many of the landscapes featured in the latter 1920s advertisements simply did not exist in the years prior. While much annexed land had come into St. Petersburg's tax rolls, additional land literally came forth from the oceans. During the heady boom years (1921–26), St. Petersburg proper expanded from eleven to fifty-three acres in size. Drastic alterations to the land occurred as developers emulated Tampa's Davis Islands and Carl Fisher's Miami Beach by scouring the bottoms of bays for salvageable sand to dredge and build upon.

Where once stood a small spoil island, often submerged at high tide, land appeared nearly overnight. C. Perry Snell, self-proclaimed pioneer land developer and donator of downtown waterfront parks, opened the upscale Snell Isle subdivision in late 1925. His promotional plan called for clubhouses, golf courses and fine homes all on a pristine yet pricey 275-acre island.

Although a rickety one-lane bridge spanned Coffee Pot Bayou and connected today's Old Northeast to what would become Snell Isle as early as 1917, the stately structure that now spans the bayou was more than a decade away.

In all actuality, the Snell Isle tract in 1917 probably had fewer than forty or fifty acres that were above sea level at the time. But then came the dredges

The very first connection to Perry Snell's exclusive residential tracts was barely crossable, but he soon turned his isle into *the* place for the well-to-do.

and dikes and the determined men and machines that transformed St. Petersburg's bays and waterfronts. Tourists-turned-buyers had their choices of hotels to pass the time during construction; however, Snell shrewdly offered accommodations (built on site) and recreation while they waited. From shuffleboard and sunbathing to unexcelled golf and gulf fishing, tourists had endless options in St. Petersburg. There were concerts in Williams Park, horseshoes and lawn bowling on just about every open public park and, for those wishing to move their card games or nightly dancing closer to water's edge, the newly created Million-Dollar Pier.

Recognizing the civic strength of the St. Petersburg's women's organization, Snell donated three lots facing Snell Isle Boulevard, where the St. Petersburg Women's Club remains today. But as Snell historian Judy Lowe Wells notes, the rickety wooden bridge frightened the women enough to campaign Snell for a sturdier replacement. The Venetian-style bridge, which complemented his grand subdivision, was erected in 1928, according to the Department of Transportation's bridges and transportation inventory. Listed as structure #157191, the T-beam concrete bridge was reconstructed in 1996 and has a daily traffic figure of nearly ten thousand vehicles.

POST-SPAN

Completed in 1928 at a cost of $1.5 million and named for a character in the renowned opera *Maritana*, Thomas Rowe's Don CeSar Hotel added a major attraction to the Gulf beaches and was considered by many as the most magnificent hotel on the Gulf of Mexico. As Pass-A-Grille developed into a social hub and resort community, Rowe's towering pink stucco and stone hotel, "the Don," became a playground for the rich and famous. From F. Scott Fitzgerald to FDR, the Mediterranean-and-Moorish-style hotel was certainly a jewel in the Gulf sands.

Although the Great Depression nearly doomed the Don, Rowe managed to secure a contract with the New York Yankees to house the team there for three consecutive springs while it trained in the Sunshine City. Rowe continued developing the surrounding blocks until his death in 1940, whereupon his wife sold the structure to the U.S. government in 1942.

During World War II, St. Petersburg experienced another significant period of growth when the U.S. Coast Guard Station at Bayboro Harbor

Presidents, athletes, movie stars and the plain old "filthy rich" relaxed and received VIP treatment at the Pink Palace—then, the War Department took over.

reopened. This installation served as a training base for thousands of seamen. At the direction of the War Department, St. Petersburg also became host to a major technical services training center for the Army Air Corps. Anti-submarine air patrols left St. Petersburg every night to survey the Gulf of Mexico. This military presence in St. Petersburg brought more than 100,000 soldiers to the area. The War Department rented hundreds of rooms at local hotels to accommodate the soldiers.

The Don CeSar also operated as a hospital for troops training in Pinellas County. Additionally, it was used as a rehabilitation center for U.S. Air Force pilots traumatized in the war, and the once opulent resort got stuck with the nickname "the Flak Hotel." In spite of the degrading moniker, significant strides were made by doctors at the Don in the documentation and better understanding of "combat fatigue" and "battle stress." The facility finally was used as a hospital for rest and relaxation thanks to its serene and peaceful beach setting. Following the war, the Don became a Veterans' Administration headquarters until 1969, when the government believed it to be obsolete. Left abandoned and considered an eyesore with peeling paint and severe interior damage, the Don faced the wrecking ball.

Thanks to a "Save the Don" crusade led by historian June Hurley Young, the "Pink Palace" was purchased by William Bowman for less than $500,000. After eighteen months and $3.5 million, the Don reopened to great fanfare in late 1973. Other interests have taken over ownership of the Pink Palace and continue renovating and refurbishing the grand structure, but the Don CeSar continues to play host to hobnobbers and the elite.

CHAPTER 3

COMPETITION FOR TOLLS

1934

Perry Snell and Thomas Rowe were just two of the many investors who knew how to make a buck. Some, like Eugene Elliott, were fast-talking, slap-you-on-the-back hucksters, while others just worked long and hard to achieve their goals.

Tampa businessman Captain Ben T. Davis knew a good deal when he saw one. Why not give old George Gandy a run for his money by offering beach-bound tourists a more direct link between Tampa and Clearwater? Charging, of course, a toll for the service: two bits one way for a car and driver plus a nickel per passenger. Without a bridge, the only land route took drivers on a thirty-mile loop through the northern community of Oldsmar, and the crossing to the south over Mr. Gandy's moneymaker was just about as far. Auto magnate Ransom E. Olds had envisioned developing the thirty-seven-thousand-acre area of the town he would name for himself on a par equal to Washington, D.C., with tree-lined boulevards leading from Tampa Bay to the center of downtown. With its own power plant and oyster shell–paved streets, Oldsmar was to be an ideal working-class community. But Ben Davis thought it was too much of a detour to get beachgoers from Tampa out to Clearwater. A shorter route—his route—was what was needed. Davis also knew what he was doing when it came to dredging, as it had become his primary business. His title of captain was earned while working out West for the Standard Dredging Co.

Davis attended the University of New Mexico, becoming one of its first engineering graduates. Fiercely proud of his ancestry as a direct descendant of Confederate president Jefferson Davis, Ben Davis came to Florida with a solid engineering reputation earned on projects in both Texas and Mexico, where he helped design that country's first practical railroad.

In 1927, he acquired the necessary Florida state clearances and made sporadic progress on his causeway for the next few years. In between paying jobs, Captain Davis kept his dredging crews busy by having them work on his own project at the northernmost end of Tampa Bay. But the Depression and the Florida land boom slowed any significant progress. Then, about five years later, pledging his construction equipment as collateral, he raised capital from friends and—most importantly—received a $600,000 loan from the Federal Reconstruction Finance Corporation. Davis was able to put men back to work, endearing him to many within the Tampa and Clearwater communities for years to come.

For a final cost of less than $1 million, he completed the northernmost crossing of Upper Tampa Bay in 1934 and named it after himself, the no-frills Ben Davis Causeway. Corita Davis, the builder's daughter, had the honor of throwing open a gate decorated with palm leaves, bougainvillea and Spanish moss, allowing a motorcade to make its way to Clearwater Beach for an afternoon celebration picnic. More than forty-five mayors and five dozen newspaper editors were invited to the festivities.

The most unique feature of the twenty-four-foot-wide roadway was the tollgate on the Pinellas side that also served as an upstairs apartment home for the Davis family. Tolls were competitive with Gandy's rates: twenty-five

Even the lonely looking Davis Causeway tollbooth was featured on a postcard for the folks back home.

cents per car and five cents per passenger. Trucks were charged by weight, while bicyclists paid five cents and motorcycles ten.

In 1979, grandson George Davis told reporters he fondly recalled watching traffic pass below him as he played in a screened-in playroom of the home. During those conversations with the press, George Davis wasn't just reminiscing; he was lobbying for the correction of what he saw as a serious injustice. He was upset with the name and fate of the causeway. As had been done elsewhere, the War Department seized the bridge, paying Davis $1.1 million and eliminating tolls as part of the war effort.

Now under state control after World War II, the causeway was renamed to honor Clearwater Beach resident and U.S. representative Courtney W. Campbell for his efforts to beautify and fund needed repairs to the causeway.

Grandson George argued that that really wasn't the case. He maintained that only a recreational area along the causeway had been named to honor Campbell and that the main thoroughfare should still carry the name of its creator, his granddaddy, Ben T. Davis. With the addition of picnic shelters

The Courtney Campbell
Causeway offers many
recreational opportunities.
Courtesy of St. Petersburg Times.

and easy access to convenient fishing areas, the roadway to the beach became a popular family destination. In 2005, it was designated by the state as an official Scenic Highway. Bikers and joggers frequently use the access roads and pedestrian paths along the popular gathering spot. In recent years, possibly due to its more remote location, police have had to investigate several shootings and gang fight incidents. But more frequent patrols have apparently helped improve the area's safety.

Traffic accidents, however, were another matter. With no posted speed limits in the early years of the Ben Davis Causeway, accidents were common. In one year, there was an average of one accident every thirty-six hours, earning the nine-mile sea-level roadway the nickname of "Suicide Alley."

Regardless of the name, it's highly unlikely that this causeway could be built today due to current environmental protection policies, and it certainly would cost more than $1 million to build. The structure altered the natural state of the extreme northern tip of Old Tampa Bay, affecting the tidal flow and the normal exchange of waters. On the positive side, the area has become a bird watcher's paradise, with dozens of species found there.

While in this extreme northwest corner of the bay, it's only fitting to at least mention the frequently ignored Bayside Bridge, which opened to traffic in 1993. Essentially running due south from Clearwater and the Courtney Campbell Causeway to Largo and the St. Petersburg/ Clearwater International Airport, this arrow-straight bridge spans only a small sector of Old Tampa Bay. However, the bridge *is* noteworthy for the way it was financed.

At an approximate cost of $75 million, it was the first major county road improvement to be paid for by the innovative "Penny for Pinellas" tax. Championed by Pinellas County administrator Fred Marquis, the Penny for Pinellas program was considered an alternative to raising property taxes. The ten-year local government sales tax was earmarked for capital improvement projects. The 1 percent tax was first approved by voters in 1989 and has been subsequently approved twice to continue until 2020. For the Bayside Bridge, it meant no toll charges and the elimination of a controversial multi-lane tollbooth that would have been constructed on eco-sensitive marshlands at the south end of the bridge.

Not all of the schemes or serious engineering concepts to span Tampa Bay came to fruition, even though some had merit. Gandy Bridge and the Sunshine Skyway, being the first and grandest, respectively, garner the most attention, but there are two more options worthy of at least an honorable mention on these pages.

In 1929, a bill was introduced in the state legislature to appropriate $7 million for the construction of a one-thousand-foot-long tunnel under Lower Tampa Bay. The submerged crossing was to be forty feet below the bottom of the bay to allow ships of any size and draft to safely and easily navigate in and out of the bay. The plan also took into account the possibility of having to dredge the shipping channel in the future to maintain acceptable depths without interfering with the tunnel.

The intended route was similar to that of the Bee Line Ferry, being more or less a straight shot between Pinellas Point and Piney Point. Tallahassee lawmakers considered granting a twenty-year lease to the West Coast Bridge and Tunnel Company with the stipulation that the franchise to operate the combination bridge/tunnel could be bought back by the state at any time at a cost-plus-10-percent price. Tampa officials generally opposed the idea of any bridges or tunnels, claiming that they would be a navigation hazard in time of war.

A lengthy and involved approval process was to have followed involving army engineers, a consortium of financial backers and, last but not least, Congress. Fuel was added to the speculative fire when army chief of staff General Charles P. Summerall made a "personal inspection tour" of the bay while reviewing a second project involving port development plans near Mullett Key. Promoters claimed the tunnel project would create a $25,000–$50,000 weekly payroll in the region for more than two years, creating a huge economic impact, especially for St. Petersburg.

By 1932, the Tunnel Company and the Bee Line Ferry Company were battling each other for $6.5 million in funding from the Reconstruction Finance Corporation. Tunnel backers again claimed the project meant 4,500 jobs and predicted that as many as 700,000 vehicles would use the tunnel annually at a toll of $1.25 each. The arguing dragged on, while overseas Adolf Hitler was formulating his plans for world domination.

Dr. Herman Simmonds, a St. Petersburg physiotherapist, had originally introduced a bridge concept in 1927, won congressional approval and received a War Department permit. But the Depression killed that dream. In March 1940, Simmonds again presented his idea for a high bridge, essentially following the ferry route. This resulted in continued squabbling with backers of the Bridge and Tunnel Company and, of course, new and higher cost/revenue/employment predictions from both sides.

County engineer Freeman Horton, of Manatee, was tapped to design a structure that would span the bay at a shorter, more westerly direction from the Pinellas Peninsula. Years later, Horton's son described the Simmonds-

Horton plan as the "Road Not Taken" in a short biographical essay about his father. Retired journalist Allan Horton suggests that had his father's design and route been chosen, there might never have been a *Summit Venture* collision with the Sunshine Skyway—a theory supported only by speculation. As fate would have it, the younger Horton was working as a reporter for the *Sarasota Herald-Tribune* and covered the deadly 1980 accident that brought down a revised version of his father's original bridge design.

Allan Horton grew up around water, boats and Florida cattle ranching, an occupation he still pursues today, along with writing some very entertaining cowboy poetry. It was only natural that he took an interest in his dad's engineering work and, for several years as a teen, helped conduct ocean-floor surveys in preparation for channel modifications and the location of the first Sunshine Skyway Bridge.

The younger Horton was interviewed in 1999 as part of a University of South Florida oral history project and spoke quite candidly about his father's recommendations that were ultimately overruled by political interests. Horton asserted that the state failed to do its job of properly maintaining the first and second generations of the Sunshine Skyway Bridge—not so much the steel and concrete structure itself, but the wooden timber "fences" that had originally been placed as bumper guards for the main piers. He contended that the state failed to replace the rotting timbers, leaving the bridge piers unprotected. And he flatly states that had the proper barriers been in place, the severity of the *Summit Venture* accident would have been averted.

Post-Span

Alfred McKethan was the right appointee at the right time to guide early progress in the state's road-and-bridge system. His native Floridian status and success as a citrus grower and banker were attributes Governor Fuller Warren took into consideration when making his selection.

In a *St. Petersburg Times* obituary, McKethan was called "a giant in the generation that built modern Florida." One fellow road board member and longtime friend said McKethan just had a way of "talking and enthusing somebody and developing ambition."

His civic and business accomplishments were diverse. He was the first chairman of the Southwest Florida Water Management District, created in 1962. Prior to that, he helped acquire the land and lay the groundwork for

Alfred Augustus McKethan
(1909–2002).

what would become Eckerd College. As chairman of the state's road board, he pushed hard for construction of the Sunshine Skyway but made another equally impressive contribution to state government—right from his desk.

After observing that very little work actually got done on Saturdays, McKethan sought permission to run his department on a five-day-per-week schedule. Governor Warren needed a little arm twisting but ultimately agreed, leading to the Saturday closure of almost all state offices.

Upon retiring, McKethan donated almost $3 million to his alma mater, the University of Florida, for the 1988 construction of a new baseball stadium now known as the Alfred McKethan Stadium at Perry Field. A year later, he wrote a history of Hernando County, Florida, entitled *Hernando County: Our Story*. His family was known for their local generosity, giving land for a county hospital and a county library and a $1 million endowment to the Pasco-Hernando Community College. McKethan died in 2002 at the age of ninety-three.

CHAPTER 4

BRIDGING THE GAP

1954

Fuller Warren was all smiles while posing for news photographers at a voting booth in the 1948 election that sent him to Tallahassee as governor.

During his four-year tenure, it was Warren who twisted arms, sought compromises and dealt with an array of agencies seeking to regulate and oversee the construction of a bridge across Lower Tampa Bay. It was also Warren who was most instrumental in securing funding for that link between Pinellas and Manatee Counties.

While governor, Warren was exposed as having once been a member of the Ku Klux Klan, but the former World War II gunnery officer denounced the group, calling them first cousins of Nazis. In spite of that claim, his successor, Daniel T. McCarty easily won the Democrat nomination and took office in 1953. After only nine months in office, he died of a massive heart attack. The remainder of McCarty's term was filled by acting governor Charley Johns, who would enjoy the distinction and credit of completing and officially opening the Sunshine Skyway Bridge.

Nevertheless, it was Fuller Warren who shouldered the principal responsibility for development of a state turnpike system and the bridging of Lower Tampa Bay. And it was a writing-cramped Fuller Warren who spent two days in a New York bonding office signing $22 million worth of bonds to finance the project. He did take a break from the mandatory signing chore to attend a Yankees baseball game. They lost.

At the time, Pinellas and St. Petersburg relied primarily on the *St. Petersburg Times* for their daily printed news, whereas Tampa residents gleaned their information from the *Tampa Tribune*. From the turn of the century, the two media outlets had been fierce rivals. Their competition for construction rights on behalf of their county was as hard fought as the battle for subscriptions. Fortunately for the *Times* and St. Petersburg, Fuller Warren and the *Tribune's* managing editor, Virgil "Red" Newton, had been bitter enemies since their college days at the University of Florida.

Neither the *Tribune* nor Warren ever had anything nice to say about the other. Because of that feud, it's likely that Governor Warren pushed for the Sunshine Skyway to connect Pinellas to Manatee County, not Hillsborough. This snub effectively eliminated any direct benefit to Newton or the *Tribune's* home county. Construction of the bridge would, however, have a huge and immediate impact on fourteen other west coast Florida counties.

By 1950, citizens of St. Petersburg were eager for bridge construction across Lower Tampa Bay to begin. They were also quite eager to promote and celebrate. And celebrate they did. On July Fourth of that year, the city hosted a blowout event billed as the "Spans Across the Bay" celebration.

Al Lang (center), the man St. Petersburg called "Mr. Baseball," being honored at the patriotic bridge celebration.

The rockets' red glare illuminated a crowd of five thousand spectators at Al Lang Field that evening, so it was fitting that Al Lang, the man credited with originally bringing baseball training to St. Petersburg, would be a guest of honor at the kickoff of the Sunshine Skyway Celebration, which featured music, speeches and fireworks.

The daylong patriotic celebration culminated with the announcement of the new name for the lower Tampa Bay Bridge, as well as the ceremonial opening of construction bids. The junior chamber of commerce received more than twenty thousand entries in a national bridge-naming contest.

Virginia Seymore of Indian Rocks, Florida, earned her fifteen minutes of fame with the winning moniker: the Sunshine Skyway Bridge. Of the top twenty-five finalists, ten used "skyway" as part of the name. As her reward, Mrs. Seymore received a key to the city from Mayor Samuel Johnson and a dedication day ride across the bridge with congressman Courtney Campbell and his wife.

By mid-October, after securing additional construction bonds, the first of many dredges and steam shovels began digging backfill for causeways. To the relief of many, the Lower Bay would be spanned.

The Virginia Bridge and Iron Company, founded in 1889, was the contractor of record for the original Sunshine Skyway span. VB&I was one of the last fabricators acquired under the American Bridge Company corporate umbrella conceived by financier J.P. Morgan. In 1901, he cobbled together twenty-four bridge and ironworks companies to control more than half of the nation's steel construction capability. Some companies on that roster retained their identities; others were absorbed under the American Bridge name. Within a year, Morgan had sold it all to the U.S. Steel Corporation. Over time, American Bridge Company's construction portfolio included New York's landmark Chrysler and Empire State Buildings, the Mackinac Bridge in Northern Michigan and San Francisco's Oakland Bay Bridge, as well as the next two generations of the Sunshine Skyway Bridge.

At a cost of $22 million, the new bridge would have an 864-foot steel girder center span, stretch four miles in length and connect six man-made causeways for a total length of fifteen miles. Sandbar and spoil areas were utilized for roadways and recreational areas at both ends of the bridge. Picnic shelters were a favorite destination for families wanting to enjoy the bay waters.

Anchored to steel pilings up to one hundred feet below the water, "one of the "world's most unusual bridges" required over three hundred men and countless tugs, barges and steam-driven rigs to complete. The massive bridge, able to endure seventy-five-mile-per-hour winds per square inch, had been designed to "withstand hurricanes of all known intensities."

As completion of the Skyway neared, the entire region started celebrating. Bathing beauty queens were selected, dignitaries and celebrities invited. Banks, bakeries and every other imaginable business bought advertising promoting Tampa Bay's newest bridge. The 1926 opening of George Gandy's bridge had created a similar attempt at promotion and advertising and included a variety of state governors and various other regional leaders—the typical collection of publicity-seeking politicians. But the Skyway fanfare would be unequalled.

Staging areas on both sides of the bay provided a steady supply of steel girders and some pre-assembled components. A complete concrete plant was established near Piney Point, and some precast concrete structures were floated by barge from a Tampa fabrication site. Though not operated like the Ganbridge company town of years gone by, the staging centers were constantly active and essential to the project moving along in a timely manner.

Once the roadway surfaces were in place, work on the causeway approaches was relatively straightforward, with cranes assisting in the pouring of concrete curbs and railings. As work progressed toward the main center span, workers and supervisors were able to drive to the job site. The occasional curiosity seeker also managed to sneak onto the bridge but was quickly herded away for safety reasons.

Reinforced concrete side rails along the causeway approaches were both an aesthetic and practical choice of the designers. It was their opinion that conventional exposed steel railings would be more susceptible to salt air corrosion and would require constant painting or touch-ups. The preformed concrete sections required some initial cleaning and anti-scaling treatment but otherwise were maintenance free.

As soon as construction crews made progress toward the center and removed their equipment, area residents and fishing buffs made their way onto the walkways—with or without permission—to see if they could land a snook or other bay water favorite.

Fishermen went about their task of enjoying the bay waters in the spring of 1953, when the Skyway's center span was finally joined. Shipping channel traffic in and out of the bay was halted while the final pieces were hoisted into place; however, the shipping lanes were reopened to freighters and other ships in less than four hours.

With steel girders in place and both ends connected, crews quickly started preparing the roadway decking. Despite the apparent lack of safety lines or barriers, construction accidents were said to be minimal. There are discrepancies in reports concerning the possible drowning of one man, and records are sketchy.

Commercial and private boats rarely had problems "shooting the gap," and if they did, the small boats—not the bridge—were the ones likely to suffer damage. The fence-like railing at the bottom of the main pier was the only collision protection from a wayward ship. It would prove to be ineffective.

With all the hoopla over naming the bridge the Sunshine Skyway, the span also carried the name of the W.E. "Bill" Dean Bridge to honor the state engineer and chief bridge designer. He was revered by his peers as the father of prestressed concrete. In 1965, just weeks after being named engineer of the year, Dean had a massive heart attack. His lifeless body was found in St. Andrews Bay under the Hathaway Bridge, a bridge he had designed, on U.S. 98 near Panama City.

Before the Skyway Bridge connected the Pinellas Peninsula to points south, there were 118,000 available rental rooms for tourists in the combined area. In just eighteen months, that number jumped by 35 percent to 160,000.

Free postcards at the front desks of many Florida motels resulted in untold thousands of dollars of advertising and promotion, often with the ubiquitous message scrawled on the back: "Having a great time, wish you were here!"

What once took over an hour was now a short ten-minute drive. Many opening-day drivers claimed bragging rights as "first across," but that feat really came months earlier on feet and seat.

It was July 1954, two months before the official Skyway Bridge opening, and *St. Petersburg Times* reporter Rube Allyn smelled a good story. Wearing their mandatory American Bridge Company hard hats, he and photographer Bob Moreland crawled and scooted across the open framework of the bridge. Snapping pictures with the Rolex camera strung from his neck, Moreland documented their journey across the bridge from end to end, staking their claim as first to cross the entire span. *Times* columnist Dick Bothwell wrote that for a number of years following the bridge crossing stunt, Allyn's shoes—which he had bronzed as a joke—hung on a wall in the *Times'* newsroom. Allyn, who had started with the *Times* as a linotype operator, had a reputation as a guy who loved a good laugh and loved fishing even more. He left the newspaper to form Great Outdoor Publishing Co. and authored many of its popular publications. Eleven editions of his *Dictionary of Fishes* were ultimately printed, selling almost one million copies. Killed in a bicycle accident at the age of sixty-seven, Allyn's last request was to be buried at sea.

Anything for a story! Scooting across the bridge and into the record books. *Courtesy of* St. Petersburg Times.

His steel-gray weighted coffin lies on the floor of the Gulf of Mexico about thirty miles off shore.

Rube Allyn and the *Times* weren't the only ones to heavily promote the benefits of the Sunshine Skyway. "The pot of gold at the end of the rainbow will be nothing compared to what this bridge will do for the economy of ten Florida west coast counties," boasted one newspaper prior to the Skyway's opening. Even though the message was heavy on hype, the end result was, in fact, huge.

The front page of the *St. Petersburg Times* Sunshine Skyway Souvenir Edition, published on September 6, 1954, reinforced the "Hands Across the Bay" theme used throughout the region. Fourteen area municipalities joined in the huge celebration, eagerly anticipating the growth opportunity the completed bridge would bring to their communities.

The Sunshine Skyway Bridge, unlike the Gandy Bridge, was viewed as the culmination of work by dozens of men throughout the region. George Gandy's project was popularly thought of as the accomplishment of a single determined man, though in truth, he had help.

St. Petersburg mayor Samuel G. Johnson and Bradenton mayor A. Sterling Hall reach out to clasp hands in a 1954 publicity photograph promoting

City mayors Sam Johnson (left) and Sterling Hall pose for bridge promotion pictures.

"Hands Across the Bay." They both knew publicity was important, and they both instinctively believed in the economic impact the Skyway would have. Immediately after the Skyway was opened, both cities saw a boost in sales tax receipts and land sales.

St. Petersburg may "look confidently to the south for a vast new market area," claimed a study by the First Research Corporation of Florida. Commissioned by the Florida State Road Department (SRD), their research predicted a 15 percent increase in retail sales and non-agricultural employment, a 22 percent boost in bank deposits and an 18 to 20 percent jump in tourist traffic. They projected that within three years of the opening of the Skyway, taxable retail figures would increase by 12 percent to more than $940 million. Their estimate was low. By 1957, it was closer to the $970 million mark.

O'Neil's Marina, located just before the Pinellas tollbooth, was one of the many retail businesses to experience an increase in sales from boaters, sightseers and fishing parties, as well as motorists stopping to ask directions.

Columnist Bothwell graphically described the opening of the Sunshine Skyway Bridge as "pulling the plug on the bottleneck to Pinellas County." The largest-capacity ferry in the Bee Line system could carry only thirty-five cars at a time—sometimes after an hour's wait. By comparison, three dozen vehicles could pay their tolls and be on their way across the bridge in less than two minutes.

Setting grudges aside, the *Tampa Tribune* declared the two-lane Skyway Bridge to be "a joint triumph of engineering and labor [that] majestically reasserts the mastery of man the planner, man the builder."

The Sunshine Skyway was composed of five bridges ranging in length from a 336-foot structure in Terra Ceia Bay to the main 864-foot steel girder center span. The total length would exceed 22,000 feet and could withstand hurricane winds of all known measurable intensities. Traffic volume predictions of 750,000 vehicles annually were quickly surpassed, reaching twice that figure by 1957.

Thousands of cars waited for hours to cross over the $22 million bridge on the toll-free opening day. The lineup brought traffic to a standstill along Thirty-fourth Street and Lakeview and Tangerine Avenues. All of these drivers and passengers would lay claim to being the first to cross. By the end of the day, tollbooth operators had counted more than fifteen thousand

Thousands waited in line on opening day for the chance to cross Tampa Bay's newest and greatest bridge.

vehicles across the new span. At 11:00 p.m., the opening day free rides across the bridge ended, and the tollbooths got down to business. St. Petersburg resident Donald Davis, on his way home from Bradenton, was the first to pay the $1.75 crossing fee at the Manatee station.

With the chamber of commerce–promised "sunny skies and beautiful bay water," opening day was a huge success, with charter busloads of spectators willing to pay for a spectacular sightseeing ride. Sam and Vivian Saporito, of Safety Harbor, waited in line for hours so they could be the first "regular citizens" to drive across the bridge. They repeated the feat in 1987 with the opening of the current Sunshine Skyway Bridge. After becoming a widower, Sam added "first-crossing" claims over the new Bayside Bridge, the Lake Seminole Bridge and, in 1995, the $15 million span at Clearwater Pass. At that event, the eighty-seven-year-old record holder said his bridge-crossing hobby was "a great way to meet women."

The open-grid steel surface of the bridge served two specific purposes. For one, it allowed air to circulate evenly above and below the bridge, thus reducing any "lift" that could occur during high winds. Secondly, the egg-

The new bridge made an impressive and majestic gateway into the bay.

crate surface weighed less than concrete and prevented any water buildup for improved vehicle traction. But for some, it was a scary or even impossible experience. The whining noise that came from tires rolling over the grid work and the fact that you could look down through the roadway to the water below was more than some folks could handle. Occasionally, drivers with a death grip on the steering wheel had to be "rescued" by bridge employees or police and driven to the shoreline. The fence-like guardrails were the only collision protection incorporated into the design to protect the bridge piers.

Amateur radio has always been called "ham radio," but these local broadcast professionals managed to ham it up for this publicity photograph after coordinating fourteen area radio stations into local "network coverage" of the bridge opening. The first local radio network included this list of stations: WTSP, WSUN and WPIN in St. Petersburg; WDAE, WFLA, WALT and WHBO in Tampa; WKXY and WSPB in Sarasota; WINK and WMYR in Fort Myers; WTRL in Bradenton; WTAN in Clearwater; WPLA in Plant City; and WBOY in Tarpon Springs. WTSP radio also became

Amidst forced yawns and a supply of NoDoz, announcers (left to right) Glenn Dill, Jim Harriott and Rich Pauley "struggle" to stay awake through the wee morning hours of round-the-clock programming timed to coincide with the Skyway dedication. Station manager Louis Brewer holds a lantern, supposedly to light up the studio. *Courtesy of* St. Petersburg Times.

the first West Florida station to go to a twenty-four-hour broadcast day, no longer required to sign off at sundown.

Compared to Gandy's gala, the Skyway dedication was a far more eclectic mix, including acting governor Charley Johns, Miss Greece and Miss Universe beauty pageant hopeful Rika Diallina, entertainer and car collector James Melton and, fresh from a cease-fire signing, former Korea commander General James Van Fleet.

This quartet of notables certainly had little in common other than name recognition. James Van Fleet, one of Harry Truman's favored military men, was in the rotation of generals charged with the enormous task of running the Eighth U.S. Army's share of what the United Nations euphemistically called a "police action" in Korea. Miss Greece, Rika Diallina (whose last name has a variety of spellings), had been a guest of the heavily Greek-populated fishing village of Tarpon Springs following her Miss Universe competition. Because of some alleged communist leanings, the beauty queen was initially denied entrance into the United States until Secretary of State John Foster Dulles stepped in to authorize visa clearance. She went on to become a favored movie star in her own country.

Dedication VIPs (left to right) James Van Fleet, Rika Diallina, James Melton and acting governor Charley Johns. *Courtesy of* St. Petersburg Times.

"America's Favorite Tenor," James Melton, was probably the best-known name on the dignitary roster. Born in Moultrie, Georgia, and raised on his parents hog farm near the small Florida community of Citra, Melton became a successful pop singer. As music tastes changed, he became an equally popular classical tenor vocalist, movie star and TV variety show host. Upon the untimely death of Governor Dan McCarty, president of the state senate Charley Johns became the Florida governor who would receive much of the recognition for completing the Sunshine Skyway. Although LeRoy Collins succeeded him as governor, Johns did not withdraw from politics, opting to return to the Senate, where he headed several controversial committees intent on uncovering communists and homosexuals in state government.

Quite likely one of Charley Johns's most enjoyable days as governor was on Labor Day 1954, when he officially opened the bridge to thousands of waiting automobiles and their excited passengers. They turned out in droves to be among the first to cross on this historic day. By midnight, fifteen thousand autos had made the inaugural trek. After leading the parade in his prized 1909 Rockwell, James Melton, a well-known car collector, drove the former New York City taxi nearly 240 miles back to his Autorama Museum in Hypoluxo, Florida, near West Palm Beach.

In addition to mandatory sunshine, another unwritten rule of Florida publicity was that bathing beauties must be present at all public events. But nobody ever seemed to object. During the opening ceremonies on the St. Petersburg side, Rika Diallina handed a replica of the Sunshine Skyway to Governor Johns, who then placed the bridge in the center of the map of Florida's west coast, symbolically linking the ten counties together. The counties—Citrus, Hernando, Pasco, Lee, Collier, Hillsborough, Pinellas, Manatee, Sarasota and Charlotte—were represented by princesses, each wearing a bright red bathing suit. The dedication attire was probably the single most obvious difference between the Skyway and Gandy's 1924 ceremonies, in which Sara Lykes Keller, Miss Tampa, and Margaret Peggy Peeler, Miss St. Petersburg—both in modest ankle-length gowns—carried out their official span-opening duties.

Prior to the speeches, James Melton led the crowd in singing the national anthem. No stranger to performing, Melton was recognized for his popular stage performance style and operatic ability. He, not Jim Nabors, was the first in 1946 to sing the familiar "Back Home Again in Indiana" at the opening of the Indianapolis 500.

A caravan of convertibles, supplied by eager Dodge dealers, carried dignitaries, reporters and guests across Tampa Bay's Sunshine Skyway Bridge on opening day, September 6, 1954. The $22-million-dollar span

Governor Johns receives a cutout model of the bridge from Miss Universe to be added to the Skyway dedication sign behind them. Sonja Opp (fourth from right) was chosen to reign as Miss Sunshine Skyway. The sixteen-year-old Miss Pinellas County was one of Doc Webb's popular poster girls. In addition to her title, she received a gift certificate, a bouquet of roses and a set of luggage. *Courtesy of* St. Petersburg Times.

connected St. Petersburg and peninsular Pinellas County, in the north, to Manatee County and other southern counties along Florida's west coast. Images of the bridge parade appeared in newspapers across the nation and, for a brief time, boosted sales for the automobile manufacturer. Despite this promotion and a host of a shattered speed and performance records in 1954 and '55, the marquee continued a downward slide for many years.

The Bee Line Ferry Company, after nearly thirty years of operation, was now obsolete. Railways and waterways could no longer accommodate travelers' demands. On that joyous "Bridge Unveiling Day of 1954," the Captains McMullen docked their respective ferries one last time and lowered their flags, signaling the end of an era. After twenty years of service with the Bee Line, Early Jr. worked briefly on the St. Johns River for another outfit before pursuing his other love—music. The elder McMullen, having spent twenty-eight long years piloting nearly fifty-three thousand trips across the bay, hung up his captain's hat for the last time. Six other Bee Line employees were among the first ten to be hired as Skyway tollbooth operators.

Well before he was elected president, Dwight Eisenhower had a serious interest in the development of a national system of interstate highways and bridges. So it was rather easy to get his endorsement of the Tampa Bay span.

In 1919, as a young lieutenant colonel, Eisenhower served as an "observer" on the army's first transcontinental motorized military convoy. Later, during World War II, he was impressed with the efficiency of the German autobahn system. Both events supported his decision as president to build the nation's interstate highway system. Shortly after the Skyway dedication, Ike told a highway safety conference:

I saw [statistics] *that in 1975…there are going to be 80 million automobiles on our streets and roads and highways. The federal government*

THE WHITE HOUSE
WASHINGTON

July 20, 1954

Dear Governor Johns:

I am delighted to learn that the Sunshine Skyway joining Pinellas and Manatee Counties has been completed.

Through the addition of this fine bridge, the new Gulf Coast road will serve to make the beautiful resorts of your State more accessible to thousands of visitors traveling by automobile, and I am sure that the bridge will be a valuable addition to our national highway program.

To you, to the State Road Board, and to all others active in this project I extend warm congratulations.

Sincerely,

Dwight D. Eisenhower

The Honorable Charley E. Johns
Acting Governor of Florida
Tallahassee, Florida

This letter from President Dwight Eisenhower, published in the Skyway dedication program, was the politically correct thing to do.

is going to do its part to build more highways and other facilities to take care
of those cars. But 80 million cars! I wonder how people will get to highway
conferences to consider the control of highway traffic.

That forecast, by the way, fell short, with 137,912,779 registered vehicles on U.S. highways in 1975.

At 10:00 a.m., once the caravan of politicos and dignitaries had made it across the bridge to the Manatee County side, the entire dedication ceremony—speeches, music, the whole ball of wax—was repeated so that residents to the south could share in the excitement.

Everyone wanted some sort of connection to the day, the event or to the bridge itself. A full-page ad in the dedication program called National Airlines an "aerial bridge to progress." In reality, National was one of the early passenger services to follow in the wake of the Benoist airboat flown by Tony Jannus. National came along in the middle of things, starting business in 1934, exactly ten years after George Gandy opened his bridge and twenty years before the first automobiles crossed the original Sunshine Skyway in

The Florida state flag on the left front fender indicates that this lead car is carrying acting governor Charley Johns and guests as they leave the tollbooth on their approach to the Sunshine Skyway Bridge. *Courtesy of* St. Petersburg Times.

1954. With a sparse fleet of two Ryan four-passenger airplanes, the flying service, based at Albert Whitted Airport, regularly crossed Tampa Bay thanks to a U.S. Mail contract between St. Petersburg and Daytona.

The brainchild of Chicago businessman Ted Baker, National Airlines actually connected the Sunshine City to sixteen other Florida cities *and* Havana, Cuba. On one very special occasion, the three-hundred-mile international flight made it possible for a couple of wealthy enthusiasts to watch the start of the famed St. Petersburg–Havana yacht race from the Municipal Pier, fly to Cuba, do a little sightseeing, light up fine cigars and wait for the winning sailors to cross the finish line near the famed Morro Castle at the entrance to Habana Harbor. However, the total number of passengers during the entire first year of National's operations was less than a third of what the Jannus brothers flew during the brief life of their airboat service.

State Road Board chairman Cecil Webb, himself an ardent fisherman, made sure that miles of catwalks would be included in the plans for the entire fifteen-mile system of bridges and causeways. These three-foot-wide walkways accommodated hundreds of anglers without crowding and provided relative safety from traffic.

Sand "splits" or spoils—strips of land created by piled-up dredged material during construction of causeways—became favorite picnic and fishing spots for residents and tourists. Promoters would boast that fifty varieties of fish were common in the waters leading into Tampa Bay. All you needed was a pole, a comfortable chair, patience and sometimes a good partner.

While automobile traffic was finally free to travel across the bridge, a special Sunshine Skyway regatta attracted boating and sailing enthusiasts from fourteen Florida west coast yacht clubs. The nearly six-hundred-foot-wide main span was more than adequate for small vessels to navigate safely but presented a far greater challenge to harbor pilots guiding freighters as long as two football fields through the dogleg channel and under the bridge.

At 11:00 p.m. the opening day free rides ended, and the tollbooths got down to business. For the next seventeen years, it was single-lane service, with traffic volume increasing annually. The 1956 addition of a second Gandy Bridge helped ease the flow, as did the 1960 completion of the W. Howard Frankland Bridge. But it was obvious to all that more lanes were needed for the Sunshine Skyway Bridge.

Even though the bridge had been under construction for several years, everyone knew it was going to shut down the Bee Line Ferry. The State Road Department was slow to react, taking nearly two months to get signs posted at the abandoned ferry docks to direct disoriented travelers to the new bridge.

A state trooper aids a motorist with a flat tire while his partner holds back traffic for safety. *Courtesy of* St. Petersburg Times.

Three U.S. Coast Guard seaplanes from Air Station St. Petersburg fly over the original Sunshine Skyway Bridge during a Gulf of Mexico search and rescue training mission. Just as the bridge replaced ferryboat service across Tampa Bay in the late 1950s, helicopters made seaplanes obsolete. These Curtis Martin P5M-1G models were the last flying boats to be used by the Coast Guard. *Courtesy of the U.S. Coast Guard.*

Heavy two-way opening day traffic totaled more than fifteen thousand automobiles. *Courtesy of* St. Petersburg Times.

Members of the Open Road Campers drew straws to determine who would lead both the north and south crossings of the Skyway Bridge.

But some business-savvy retailers didn't mind, offering "Free Sunshine Skyway Information" inside in hopes of attracting customers. However, auto clubs, civic leaders and local businesses continued to ask the district engineer's office for more signs.

For some travelers, the Sunshine Skyway was more than a connection to the south. It was a destination. One particular caravan of truck campers picked St. Petersburg as a vacation spot just so they could make a group crossing of the span. An overnight bivouac near Sarasota was followed by a few days of exploring the Tamiami Trail

With the original Sunshine Skyway Bridge providing a dramatic background, three Cypress Gardens beauties perform their trademark pyramid stunt. Produced well before the advent of computers and digital cameras, this full-page special section of the *Evening Independent* convincingly combined a photograph of the bridge with a second shot of the gals in perfect pyramid pose. The popular Florida ski team did spend several days in the Tampa Bay area promoting the new bridge for newsreel cameras—just not this exact shot. *Courtesy of* St. Petersburg Times.

On September 6, 1954, veteran news photographer Bob Preston captured this un-retouched transportation evolution scene of a modern Coast Guard helicopter hovering over the nation's longest bridge while the obsolete *Manatee* ferry plied the bay waters below for the last time. *Courtesy of Patricia Preston Warren.*

and the Everglades. Then, drivers in the Open Road camper group drew straws to see who would win the honor of leading the road gypsies on the return trip across the bay.

Post-Span

General James Van Fleet, former Eighth U.S. Army commander in Korea, was chosen as the Skyway dedication keynote speaker. Six months earlier, upon his retirement, President Harry Truman had called Van Fleet "the greatest general we have ever had. I sent him to Greece, and he won the war. I sent him to Korea, and he won the war." It was a slight exaggeration on Harry's part, since fighting in Korea ended with a stalemate truce that is still in effect today and occasionally politically poked by North Korea in an attempt to flex its muscles. Van Fleet is given credit for establishing the Korean Military Academy and other officer training programs for the South Korean Forces in an effort to strengthen the republic's military against further enemy aggression. The New Jersey native who grew up in Florida returned home a highly decorated hero.

James Alward Van Fleet (1892–1992).

Van Fleet's grandfather served in the New York Militia during the Revolutionary War, and his mother and father were personal friends of Abraham Lincoln. The younger Van Fleet's first military action came under the command of General "Black Jack" Pershing during the Mexican Revolution pursuit of Pancho Villa. He then served in both world wars and was twice awarded the Silver Star for bravery. His twenty other military decorations include the Distinguished Service Cross (with two oak leaf clusters), the Purple Heart and the Combat Infantryman's Badge.

Today, the General James A. Van Fleet State Trail, a twenty-nine-mile course through the Green Swamp, is named in his honor. A West Point classmate of Generals Omar Bradley and Dwight Eisenhower, Van Fleet was featured on two covers of *Time* magazine but never shared his peers' huge name recognition status. He does, however, lay claim to one accomplishment over both Omar and Ike. Between the wars, during the 1923–24 college football seasons, he was head coach of the Florida Gators, achieving a two-year record of 12-3-4. He died at the age of one hundred on his Polk County ranch and is buried in Arlington National Cemetery.

CHAPTER 5
TIMELINE

1888: In June, the Orange Belt Railroad brings goods and northern visitors to the Pinellas Peninsula, chugging around Tampa Bay.

1903: Three steamers operated by the Independent Steamship Company begin daily service, carrying passengers between St. Petersburg and Tampa.

1914: Pilot Tony Jannus initiates a new industry, flying the world's first regularly scheduled passenger flight from St. Petersburg to Tampa on New Year's Day.

1915: The Indian Rocks Beach Toll Bridge is completed at a cost of $7,500.

1921: McAdoo Bridge is destroyed by hurricane winds and water.

1924: Gandy Bridge, "the world's longest toll bridge," opens November 20, providing the first east–west link between St. Petersburg and Tampa.

1926: Bee Line Ferry begins operating on February 24, with one boat, the *Fred D. Doty*, making five round trips daily between Bradenton and St. Petersburg.

1927: Jack Corey completes his thirty-foot-wide span over Boca Ceiga Bay.

1934: Newsreel cameras record the dedication of the Davis Causeway linking Tampa to Clearwater as the northernmost span across Old Tampa Bay.

1947: Twenty-seven Bee Line Ferry employees stage a brief wage strike on October 25. The National Labor Relations Board refuses to intervene.

1948: The Davis Causeway is renamed for Clearwater resident and U.S. representative Courtney W. Campbell, a leader in roadway beautification efforts.

1950: On October 19, the Atlantic Dredging Co., of Satsuma, Florida, begins pumping sand from the bay floor in preparation for the Skyway Bridge.

1954: The north–south Sunshine Skyway link is connected. The final girder is riveted into place on July 1. Work crews take a five-minute celebration break.

1954: The four-mile-long Sunshine Skyway Bridge opens on September 6 between Manatee and Pinellas Counties. The Bee Line Ferry ends operations.

1956: Construction of a second Gandy Bridge parallel to the first route is completed.

1960: W. Howard Frankland Bridge opens on January 15 but closes the next day due to traffic jams. Poor design earns it the nickname "Frankenstein Bridge."

1971: A twin two-lane Sunshine Skyway Bridge is added on May 19 as a southbound span. The original Skyway now carries northbound traffic only.

1975: A third Gandy Bridge opens parallel to the 1956 span.

1980: U.S. Coast Guard buoy tender *Blackthorn* capsizes near the Skyway Bridge. The loss of twenty-three crew members is the worst peacetime loss in Coast Guard history.

1980: Thirty-five people die on May 9 when the freighter *Summit Venture* strikes a pier of the "new" 1971 southbound Skyway Bridge during a severe storm.

1980: The undamaged northbound Skyway Bridge reopens on May 11 and reverts to single-lane two-way traffic.

1981: Governor Bob Graham calls for the state to build a replacement Skyway Bridge. He is recognized as one of the strongest proponents of a new span.

1987: Fifteen thousand runners participate in a January 11 pre-opening run across the new $244 million Sunshine Skyway.

1987: A cable-supported "third-generation" Sunshine Skyway opens on April 30. The new span is 50 percent wider and protected by huge bumpers called "dolphins."

1990: First- and second-generation Sunshine Skyway spans (1954 and 1971) are demolished for salvage. Portions of the causeways are kept as fishing piers.

1993: Bayside Bridge in northernmost Old Tampa Bay opens in June. The span is built with funds from the Penny for Pinellas alternative tax program.

1995: A new westbound Gandy Bridge opens, and the 1975 span is closed. Hillsborough and Pinellas County officials consider a pedestrian-only bridge.

1999: The idle 1975 Gandy Bridge, renamed Friendship Trail Bridge, officially opens as one of the world's longest pedestrian-only bridges and offers jogging, bicycling, skating and fishing.

1999: The Sunshine Skyway Bridge becomes the first in nation to install solar-powered telephones providing a direct link to crisis center counselors in an effort to reduce suicide attempts.

2005: The state legislature honors former governor and U.S. senator Bob Graham by renaming the Skyway bridge in his honor. Courtney Campbell Causeway is designated as an official Scenic Highway.

2007: The Florida Department of Transportation gives Sunshine Skyway Bridge a satisfactory health index rating but confirms evidence of some concrete erosion.

2011: Both road and water traffic move more efficiently following the completion of a $70 million renovation to John's Pass Bridge.

2012: Former governor Charlie Crist unveils the U.S. Postal Service stamp featuring Dan Cosgrove's illustration of the Sunshine Skyway Bridge.

2012: Preservationists win a demolition delay of Friendship Trail Bridge; park options to be explored.

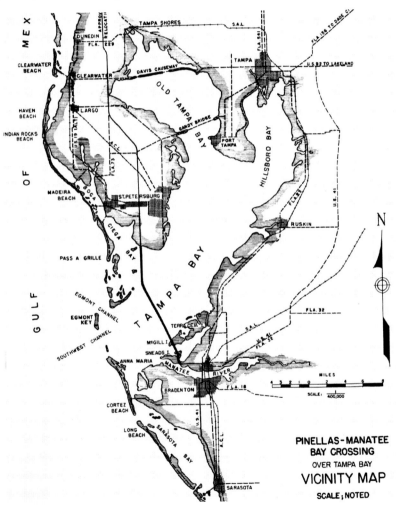

A 1945 Tampa Bay map published in a preliminary bridge engineering report that was ultimately rejected.

CHAPTER 6

THE MID-BAY AND A TWIN

1957

In April 1957, a month before bids were opened, Senator Paul Kickliter of Tampa convinced fellow lawmakers to rename what they called the "Mid-Bay Bridge" the W. Howard Frankland Bridge, in honor of the man who proposed it. Frankland, a Tampa businessman, was a former State Road Board member and wielded considerable influence through his position on the Turnpike Authority. Former Road Board chairman Alfred McKethan, an equally influential and effective leader, said the estimated $11 million cost for the proposed mid-bay span was out of line and could not be fully paid for by tolls. McKethan further argued that an additional Gandy Bridge, parallel to the existing one, was a much better alternative and could be built for about one-third the cost. However, Frankland and his supporters prevailed with the new crossing, and its approaches were completed at a final cost of more than $16 million. McKethan would later see his "expansion of Gandy" argument upheld—with four upgrades. But on January 16, 1960, the dedication of Tampa Bay's newest crossing was a family affair. Frankland was reunited with his four brothers to watch as his wife christened the span. Then, granddaughters Winifred, eight, and Jennifer, six, helped toddler W. Howard Frankland II with the ribbon-cutting duties.

That ribbon-cutting ceremony proved to be one of the few safe things that would happen for a number of years on the causeway. At least the kids didn't run with their scissors.

The original Frankland causeway proved to be a testament to poor design, lacking emergency shoulders, incorporating unusual grading and sporting a median that seemed to magnetically draw cars into the center lane. Designers drafted unusual approach routes and small navigation channels that helped create part of the problem. Shutting down the bridge one day after the grand opening should have been a clue of what was to come. Neither the Tampa nor St. Petersburg ends had adequate entrance or exit points, resulting in an instant bottleneck at both ends. Nicknamed the "Frankenstein," accidents were common. By 1962, ten fatalities had been recorded before a reinforced concrete center barrier was finally added to prevent crossover head-on collisions.

Affirming the concept of bridges tying communities together, an *Evening Independent* editorial asserted that the new Frankland Bridge would have a major impact on St. Petersburg, "into the heart of which, somehow, an extension of the big expressway must be built." The newspaper also predicted that "if carefully chosen," an expressway system "should also wipe out some presently depressed areas," thus giving an extra federal assist to urban renewal.

The 1960 opinion essay stressed that political bickering had delayed the much-needed mid-bay crossing between the rival towns for more than three decades. Nevertheless, the editorial had praise for the work of one specific individual in developing the much-maligned original Frankland Bridge. Still, a double-capacity Gandy structure, in their opinion, could not be asked to take on the special functions of an interstate highway terminal section. "Many have contributed," the essay proclaimed, "but special note must be made of the heavy contribution by Al Rogero of Clearwater, State Road Board member for this district."

Over the next decade, Florida's population continued to explode. Never-ending commuter and tourist activity made it evident that a single two-lane Sunshine Skyway Bridge across Lower Tampa Bay would not be sufficient. In February 1971 alone, 341,921 vehicles crossed the single span, producing $176,323 in tolls—a 10 percent increase from the previous year.

Designed by the Florida Department of Transportation, the new Skyway span would shuttle two lanes south while the earlier structure would provide two-lane, northbound-only operations. Hugging tight and mimicking each curve of the original bridge, the new crossing was initially planned to open in 1969, but due to a quarter-inch gap that was nearly twenty feet long, the bridge was delayed. At a cost of $25 million and fifty-four months of construction, the nearly identical sister of the Sunshine Skyway opened on May 19, 1971.

Although opening ceremonies paled in comparison to the first span's 1954 grand celebration, dignitaries and drivers watched as Governor Reubin Askew pronounced the bridge open and received the key to the city of St.

Construction of the Skyway twin was going smoothly until a quarter-inch crack was discovered, delaying completion for nearly two years.

Petersburg from Mayor Herman Goldner. The Lakewood High School Band played "America the Beautiful"—a tribute from sea to shining sea, no doubt. Benedictions on the Manatee side an hour later concluded the festivities.

In a sense, the bridges and causeways of Tampa Bay are like living entities, going through cycles of creation, expansion, decay, duplication and replacement. This has been the case with virtually all of the crossing spans and will continue to be so as is illustrated by the Howard Frankland Bridge that has surpassed the fifty-year mark. Long-range talk of a replacement has even included the addition of light rail, but that's a long way in the future.

In the years that followed the completion of the second-generation Sunshine Skyway, tourists by the millions would roll into Florida. Some were there to visit aging parents who, no doubt, felt they had earned a few years of the good life in sunny St. Petersburg before the pearly gates swung open. Some came for the surf and sun and the stories to tell back home. And others, many others, were there to visit the house of the mouse. Disney had recently come to Florida and set up a trap of his own near Orlando. Its roads led to the Atlantic and Gulf shores, and vice versa.

More bridges meant more money.

Construction on the second Skyway span moved smoothly through the mid-1960s. The procedures were identical to those used to build the first span. The same staging areas on shore, the same prestressed concrete piers and beams and, unfortunately, the same seafloor bore samples. Engineers overlooked sea-bottom characteristics for the second span's main pier support. As it turned out, the bedrock under portions of the new span was not as dense as it was under the first bridge. The resulting crack delayed construction and bumped the price tag to just under $25 million when the twin opened that day in May 1971.

Studies would later indicate that the gap had occurred due to the settling of a twelve-thousand-ton pier in the unexpected sand bed. Bracing and major repairs to the south channel pier were performed on the steel pilings. Before the Florida Department of Transportation officially opened the new companion span, an additional two years were spent on repairs and $3 million added to the already hefty price tag.

Delays seemed to be a common theme with the much-needed bridge. Even though the new 1971 span was to be used by southbound traffic following its opening, motorists were forced to use only one lane for the next month. The other lane was occupied by air compressors and painting equipment. High winds had slowed down the bridge's final painting needs. A crew of seventeen worked seven days a week until mid-June to complete the task of covering the superstructure with protective aluminum paint.

Ten Gulf Coast counties benefited from the Skyway in both tourism and population growth. Florida's population over the next decade continued to explode. The toll remained at the lowered 1966 price of fifty cents.

Forty years prior, when the Bee Line Ferry had begun operations, St. Petersburg was home to fewer than forty thousand residents. Hand-laid bricks with granite curbs lined the streets, and tent cities spotted the city. Before the 1971 completion of the second Skyway span, the population had grown to a quarter of a million. By 1970, almost 3.5 million vehicles had passed over the bay, depositing enough pocket change in tolls to repay the original bridge bonds four years earlier than projected.

At the same time, Tampa Bay's Intracoastal waters played host to major international trade. Set up as a foreign trade zone, Port of Tampa traffic was more diverse than Disney's Epcot Center. From citrus to phosphate, Florida products were exported by freighter to worldwide destinations. Traffic under and over the Sunshine Skyway rose dramatically. Though it didn't receive nearly the commercial or political prominence showered on the original span, the twin bridge saw automobile counts almost double in less than one year. By the time the second bridge opened, the traffic count, like the price, had increased as well. In 1972, the total was a staggering 3,974,834 vehicles.

By 1978, engineers, state officials and the general public all agreed that a larger-capacity replacement of the mid-bay Frankland Bridge was needed. Finally, in 1988, construction of a new $54 million span was begun, opening to traffic two years later. The old bridge was closed, rehabilitated and reopened in 1992. The entire eight-lane span, now a part of I-275, had four northbound and four southbound lanes.

The Sunshine Skyway was added to Pinellas County's list of state wildlife refuges in June 1965 while construction was underway on the twin span.

Audubon Society members and state wildlife personnel lend a hand in erecting signs designating lands near the bridge as wildlife refuge areas. *Courtesy of* St. Petersburg Times.

Representatives of the local and state Audubon Society and the Florida Game and Fresh Water Fish Commission erected the signs at each end of the Sunshine Skyway. The refuge takes in portions of Pinellas, Hillsborough and Manatee Counties. The areas were set aside to protect the state's wildlife.

On the recreation side of things, the spans were a fisherman's paradise. Snook, mackerel and barnacle-loving sheepshead were in abundance. It was not unusual for a boat moored to the main channel pilings to haul in two hundred pounds or more of sheepshead in a day's outing.

The U.S. Coast Guard added additional navigational markers to the ship channel as an aid to pilots aiming huge vessels in and out of the dogleg harbor. The devices are off-limits to civilians except in cases of emergency. Today's Global Positioning Systems (GPS) are more reliable and accurate in guiding approaching ships, but the navigation lights are still used today as well.

POST-SPAN

Frequently called "Reubin the Good" by supporters who admired his personal integrity, Governor Reubin Askew did more for Florida than just officiate the ceremonial opening of the Skyway "twin" span in 1971.

Reubin Askew. *Courtesy of* St. Petersburg Times.

In 1974, Askew became the first governor in Florida history to be elected to a second consecutive four-year term. One of his most significant "Sunshine"-related efforts came in 1976 when the legislature refused to act on a bill requiring full financial disclosure by public officials. Known as the Sunshine Amendment, Askew took his cause straight to the voters. He garnered more than 220,000 petition signatures to force the measure onto the ballot, resulting in an 80 percent margin of victory. Retired in 1979 from state government, Askew served in Jimmy Carter's cabinet. Later, he became the first Floridian to run for president of the United States. But a last-place finish in the 1984 New Hampshire primary prompted him to direct his energies toward higher education.

In 1988, Askew was selected as Florida State University's Most Outstanding Alumnus of the Century by the National Association of State Universities and Land Grant Colleges. He began his teaching career in 1989 at Florida International University, later teaching at Florida Atlantic University, the University of Florida and Florida State University, where the School of Public Administration and Policy is named in his honor. In 1992, he was named a fellow of the congressionally chartered National Academy of Public Administration. He holds honorary doctorates from FSU, UF, Notre Dame, the University of Miami and ten other universities.

Some of Askew's other notable and then-controversial accomplishments during his eight-year tenure include the appointment of Joseph W. Hatchett as Florida's first black Supreme Court justice and the appointment of the state's first black post–Reconstruction cabinet member, Secretary of State Jesse J. McCrary Jr. He guided studies on affirmative action within state government, calling for equal pay for minority groups and women. He was also an outspoken advocate for compliance with federal laws requiring bussing of school students.

CHAPTER 7

A COAST GUARD TRAGEDY

1980

The freighters that carried massive amounts of cargo in and out of the Port of Tampa often passed luxury cruise liners with their special cargo of cash-carrying tourists. Combine this volume of traffic with sheer navigation difficulty brought about by geography and weather and the result is a shipping channel with a history of several maritime disasters. This busy international port, positioned within the shallow waters of Tampa Bay, is one of the longest shipping channels in the world and one of the most difficult to navigate—even more so in a blinding squall.

While out repairing navigational markers two miles south of the Sunshine Skyway Bridge, the U.S. Coast Guard buoy tender *Blackthorn*, blinded by the bright lights of the approaching Russian cruise ship *Kazakhstan*, collided with the oil tanker *Capricorn*.

On January 28, 1980, at 8:20 p.m., the two massive ships slammed into each other. During the collision, the *Capricorn*'s seven-ton anchor embedded in the buoy tender's hull. When the 990-foot anchor chain ran its length, the *Blackthorn* was pulled back with a violent force, capsizing the tender in less than ten minutes. Some seamen were tossed into the ship channel like toy dolls. Others had to clamor up ladders or rails seeking safety or a jumping platform. Some in the crew of fifty were trapped below deck.

Seaman Apprentice Billy Flores, nineteen, was fresh out of boot camp. The *Blackthorn* was his first sea duty; it would also be the young Texan's last. As the ship was capsizing, his shipmates yelled at him to jump, but according to official records, Flores managed to make his way to a locker on the starboard side of the sinking ship and began throwing lifejackets to men

A U.S. Coast Guard buoy tender prepares for a mission. *Courtesy of* St. Petersburg Times.

already in the water. He remained on the inverted hull, giving immediate aid to several confused and injured shipmates. Flores then returned to the life jacket storage locker. Continuing to ignore shouts to save himself and jump, his final act was to tie open the locker lid with his own belt so that more life vests might float to the surface.

Rescue parties were able to get to the scene quickly to provide help. Fortunately, for those who managed to escape the sinking ship, water temperatures that night were reported as moderate, thus reducing the onset of hypothermia. The anguished faces and blank stares of survivors told the story of the *Blackthorn*: twenty-three of the ship's fifty crewmen perished, but the selfless actions of Flores saved these two men plus twenty-five others.

Chilled and wet but alive, many of the surviving crewmen quite possibly owed their lives to a young hero. The capsizing of the buoy tender was recorded as the worst peacetime disaster in Coast Guard history. The bodies of all twenty-three who perished were recovered successfully.

Tampa Port Authority officials stationed on the nearby twin spans watched the disabled oil carrier being maneuvered by tugboats the day after the collision. Freeing the disabled oil tanker *Capricorn* after her collision

The agony of losing shipmates was obvious as this *Blackthorn* survivor was comforted. *Courtesy of* St. Petersburg Times.

with *Blackthorn* was a relatively routine maritime maneuver but did require a team of five harbor tugs. The Tampa Bay shipping channel was closed to traffic for only a few hours but remained obstructed by the sunken Coast Guard cutter for several weeks.

Following the raising of the Coast Guard tender and the recovery of bodies from the wreckage, a maritime board of inquiry included Florida Port Authority and Coast Guard officials, as well as National Transportation Safety Board representatives. Primary responsibility for the collision was ultimately placed with Lieutenant Commander George Sepel because he had permitted an inexperienced junior officer to navigate the ship in an unfamiliar waterway with heavy traffic.

Recovery of the *Blackthorn* took several weeks, but the 180-foot ship was brought to the surface so a full accident investigation could be carried out. Later, authorities ruled out an expensive rebuild of the vessel. The vessel was stripped of copper and other salvageable materials and sunk as an artificial reef in the Gulf of Mexico.

A monument commemorating both the sinking of the *Blackthorn* and the loss of twenty-three coast guardsmen is now located at the Sunshine Skyway Bridge north-end rest area. The marker is inscribed with the Coast Guard's motto, *Semper Paratus* ("Always Ready") and includes the names of those who perished. A memorial service is held annually at the site.

The *Blackthorn*'s bow anchor and a granite marker are part of a permanent memorial to one of the most devastating U.S. Coast Guard losses in history. Each year, the solemn memorial service conducted at the quiet marker site is interrupted only by the single clang of a ship's bell as the name of each of the perished crew members is read aloud and unanswered.

For unknown reasons, it took twenty years, but finally, at a September 16, 2000, graveside ceremony, a proud Texas family was presented with a parchment folder bearing a gold seal and the following engraved inscription: FLORES, William R., Seaman Apprentice, USCG.

Flores was posthumously awarded the Coast Guard Medal, the service's highest peacetime award for heroism. The citation reads in part, "His exceptional fortitude, remarkable initiative·and courage throughout this tragic incident were instrumental in saving many lives and resulted in the sacrifice of his own life."

POST-SPAN

In 2011, the U.S. Coast Guard christened the first fourteen of fifty-eight high-tech Fast Response Cutters (FRCs) designed to patrol the nation's ninety-five thousand miles of coastline and fifty thousand miles of navigable waters. Each Sentinel-class ship is named in honor of a Coast Guard enlisted hero. The third 154-foot craft to be commissioned into service was the USCGC *William Flores*.

Initially, the cutter has been home-ported in the Miami/Key West sector with a crew of twenty-four. Coast Guard commandant Admiral Bob Papp says, "The FRCs will become key workhorses, carrying out coastal security patrols, search and rescue and national defense missions."

At its launching ceremony, several survivors publicly told the Flores family members present that "Billy" had no doubt saved their lives. "I barely had my head out of the water when a loose life vest floated right in front of me," one survivor said. "It had to be from that [storage] locker he tied open to save some of us."

The USCGS *William Flores,* launched October 2011. *Courtesy of the U.S. Coast Guard.*

The official coat of arms honors not only the perished crew members with the numeral twenty-three on a navigation buoy but also the Sunshine Skyway Bridge. The heraldry design with sprigs of the blackthorn tree symbolizing the strength needed to persevere in the face of adversity commemorates the USCGC *Blackthorn.*

Chapter 8

THE BRIDGE IS DOWN

1980

Nearly three months after the *Blackthorn* disaster, on a dreary May morning, strong winds and rains pelted Tampa Bay. Just after sunrise, harbor pilot John Lerro boarded the Liberian-registered *Summit Venture* in order to navigate the ship from the mouth of Tampa Bay under the two massive sister spans and into the Port of Tampa.

The six-hundred-foot freighter had come empty from the Port of Houston, where it had unloaded its freight of Japanese steel and was scheduled to pick up twenty-seven tons of phosphate destined for South Korea. The *Summit Venture* rode high in the water and continued to head into the channel. Rapidly, all visibility and radar were lost—the ship was at the mercy of Mother Nature. The tall sides of the ship acted as a sail and continued pushing the vessel off course. The storm became so blinding that Captain Lerro overshot his bearings by eight hundred feet. The result was catastrophic.

The bow of Captain Lerro's ship veered out of the channel and struck a support column on the southbound span's support pier at 7:34 a.m., resulting in a horrendous collapse of the 1971 main span. Several automobiles, a pickup truck and one Greyhound bus soared at nearly seventy miles an hour into the bay 150 feet below. Thirty-six people fell into the bay that day. All but one died.

"Mayday! Mayday! Mayday!" Captain Lerro shouted into his radio. "The Skyway Bridge is down—stop the traffic!" The freighter's crew scrambled to assist those in the water. The squall had subsided, and visibility was now restored. The carnage was shocking. Amidst the showering debris of concrete and steel, only one survivor was plucked from the bay that tragic morning. The Mayday radio calls quickly rallied emergency vessels to the disaster scene.

Divers from the Eckerd College search and rescue team in St. Petersburg were among the first on the scene. Soon, Coast Guard personnel and nearby civilians frantically searched for bodies, pulling them aboard their rescue boats. Periodic rainsqualls hampered recovery efforts. Meanwhile, a makeshift morgue was set up at nearby Mullet Key.

Richard Hornbuckle's 1976 Buick rests where it skidded to a stop just fourteen inches from the edge of the collapsed portion of the bridge. He and his three passengers

The bow of the *Summit Venture* strewn with steel girders from the bridge above. *Courtesy of* St. Petersburg Times.

worked for a St. Petersburg automobile wholesaler and were headed north on the bridge to pick up three cars in Avon Park. Hornbuckle and his front seat passenger, Jim Crispin, managed to evacuate the car in a daze, with backseat riders Kenneth Holmes and Anthony Gattus close behind, gripping the steel roadway for traction. Hornbuckle told a TV reporter that after he and his pals "bailed out" and went down the roadway to warn other drivers, he cautiously returned to his car and closed all four doors that had been left open. "I was afraid the wind was going to blow it over the edge," he said. His friend Anthony Gattus disagreed, claiming that Hornbuckle returned to rescue his golf clubs from the trunk of his precariously perched car.

In addition to special editions covering the disaster, newspapers throughout the Suncoast region, led by the *St. Petersburg Times*, immediately began asking

Richard Hornbuckle somehow stopped just inches from the edge of the collapsed Sunshine Skyway Bridge. *Courtesy of* St. Petersburg Times.

for answers to safety questions. Some claimed the bridge was jinxed, but most editorials pointed to numerous "near misses" that should have served as warnings of the impending disaster.

Though the collision was a shock, it did not come as a total surprise. Previous near misses had already begun establishing a pattern of when, not if. The first warning of a direct hit on the Sunshine Skyway Bridge came in 1978. The *Phosphore Conveyor*—at the time the world's second-largest bulk carrier—lost power as it approached the bridge. The ship's pilot managed to stop it just forty feet short of colliding with the structure by deploying the anchor and reversing engines. On February 16, 1980, the freighter *Thalassini Mana* was entering the Port of Tampa when its jumbo boom struck Skyway's southbound center span, ripping away pieces of steel. Repairs to the structure cost $19,000 and closed one traffic lane for two weeks. The incident occurred while the sunken *Blackthorn* blocked the ship channel.

The most serious accident, which happened just three months before the *Summit Venture* collision, involved the 720-foot *Jonna Dan*, piloted by John Lerro. Investigators said Lerro over-corrected when trying to avoid the wreckage of the *Blackthorn*, which still blocked the ship channel. He ordered the *Jonna Dan* to drop anchor to stop the ship, but winds pushed the stern into the bridge, breaking out about $40,000 worth of concrete chunks.

Many felt that Lerro was an experienced captain who should have known better than attempt to navigate the tricky dogleg channel during a torrential downpour, but a formal hearing found no fault with the harbor pilot's actions. Surprisingly, the National Transportation Safety Board concluded that "the probable cause of the accident was the unexpected encounter with severe weather involving high winds and heavy rain." Marine Board records indicate that Lerro had seven accidents during his first forty-two months as a Tampa Bay harbor pilot. He returned to piloting harbor ferries. Lerro's wife said that he was tormented by a daily memory of the fatal *Summit Venture* collision, once telling reporters, "If I had my life to do over again, I'd be a flute player." He died of multiple sclerosis on August 31, 2002. He was fifty-nine.

The horrible reminder of lives lost and $35 million in lost revenue per day was more than enough pressure for the Port of Tampa and the State of Florida to clear the channel in just over two weeks. The cleanup cost the state nearly $5 million.

The *Summit Venture* bow was covered with a mass of twisted steel girders and fallen chunks of concrete from the Sunshine Skyway Bridge following

Amazingly, none of the *Summit Venture* crew was injured, despite a freighter covered with twisted steel beams from above. *Courtesy of* St. Petersburg Times.

the fatal collision. Amazingly, none of its crew was seriously injured, and they tried in vain to aid with rescue attempts. Wes MacIntire, the sole survivor, had been lucky—if you could call careening from a bridge and plummeting into the bay "luck." His falling pickup truck landed on the bow of the freighter, softening the impact before toppling into the bay. Ironically, the ship that caused the needless death and massive destruction that morning had helped save him. A shroud of mystery followed him the rest of his life, for few had ever gone over the side of the Skyway and lived to tell the tale.

The Greyhound bus headed for Miami and six other southbound automobiles were not as fortunate. The steel and aluminum of this rolling coffin was torn to shreds as it slammed into the hard, cold waters. Blunt trauma from the sudden plunge into the bay killed most passengers on impact. The remaining victims perished by drowning. The thirty-five victims, now a part of the deadly history of Tampa Bay, were all recovered and laid to rest.

It wasn't until 1984 that all of the wrongful death lawsuits in the disaster were tried or settled. Damages awarded from trials averaged $300,000. MacIntire received $175,000 from owners of the shipping line.

Each of the twin spans was insured for $57 million by National American Insurance Co., headquartered in Nebraska. The company paid most of the cost of removing more than 2,300 tons of debris from the channel, according to Dewey Oliver, the FDOT engineer in charge of the cleanup operation.

A local wrecker operator used a 75-foot chain and 150 feet of cable to successfully retrieve Richard Hornbuckle's car from the edge of the bridge—but not without help. Neither Bob DeMond nor his truck stop helper could swim, and both were more than just a little intimidated by the 150-foot drop-off to the sea below. So a fireman wearing a life jacket and tethered by a safety line attached the tow cable to the car for them.

The *Summit Venture* would be recorded among the worst bridge accidents in U.S. history. Other tragic bridge disasters include the November 1972 accident in Brunswick, Georgia, in which ten people died in the Brunswick River when a freighter rammed the Sidney Lanier Bridge and a 1964 accident near New Orleans in which six passengers were killed when their Continental Trailways bus dropped through a gap in the Lake Pontchartrain Bridge after two runaway barges rammed the twenty-four-mile-long span.

When the 1971 sister span of the Sunshine Skyway was brought down by the *Summit Venture* collision, the older, original 1954 northbound thoroughfare reverted to providing two-way traffic across the bay. And once again, Dad Gandy's bridge became an important link to destinations south of Tampa

With half a bridge sitting on the ocean floor, leaving a 180-foot gap, this highway department warning sign qualifies as the ultimate understatement. *Courtesy of* St. Petersburg Times.

Bay. For the first few days following the crash, the remaining original bridge was kept closed by officials.

Once the original 1954 bridge returned to two-way traffic service, some area residents, including ferry captain Early McMullen, petitioned for a temporary return of ferry service, but to no avail. The Florida Department of Transportation converted the remaining approaches of the downed span into the "world's longest fishing pier." A crossover was added between the two original approaches to make the fishing pier accessible by foot or car, with plenty of parking. One sportswriter called the selection of fish now living in the reefs "a virtual smorgasbord of aquatic life."

Salvage teams managed to clear the ship channel of debris to at least allow vital cargo traffic to exit and enter the Port of Tampa. But in Tallahassee, politicians, planners and engineers were holding both public and private sessions to determine the next step. The biggest question was, "Repair or replace?"

The answer to replace came fairly quickly, but it would be more than a decade before the original twin steel bridges would be demolished.

By early 1990, bridge-mounted overhead cranes had begun removing sections of steel from both ends of the damaged span. By this time, the center span steel had been removed from the original Skyway Bridge, and traffic was flowing on the new cable-supported bridge. After girders were cut, four 250-ton hydraulic cranes were used to lower this large portion of the damaged bridge to barges waiting below. This engineering and navigational ballet was accomplished in less than three hours, allowing ship channel traffic to resume quickly. The section was then cut apart in a salvage yard. The remaining concrete piers were blown up, with chunks settling to the bottom as a new artificial reef. Once completed, the converted southern fishing pier would extend farther than its northern counterpart. With plenty of parking and no closing time, the fishing piers would quickly become a fisherman's dream and another lucrative tourist drawing card for the region.

Over several decades, a handful of collisions to the other bay bridges have been reported, but most have been what might be called fender benders, involving small fishing trawlers or pleasure craft. None has resulted in major structural damage or lives lost. But with a continually increasing volume of cargo traffic through Tampa Bay, other dangers exist—specifically from oil or chemical spills.

In 1993, one of the most spectacular accidents of this type took place just south of the Sunshine Skyway Bridge near Egmont Key. A four-hundred-foot freighter named *Balsa 37*, carrying a six-thousand-ton load of phosphate headed for Columbia, was sinking. Meanwhile, a disabled fuel barge near the Skyway was oozing its load of eight thousand barrels of fuel oil toward the eastern shore, and the seagoing *Ocean 255* fuel barge was a burning inferno. The three vessels had somehow collided, causing the chaotic scene. Amazingly, no bridge damage was reported. Only two of the nearly three dozen crewmen involved sustained minor injuries, and quick response by spill containment crews kept shoreline damage to a minimum. Governor Lawton Chiles repeatedly emphasized to the press, "We don't have an *Exxon Valdez* on our hands here," referring, of course, to the 1989 Alaska oil spill disaster. However, at the time—and still today—some "experts" claim that such an event in Tampa Bay is a when-not-if proposition, warning that adequate precautions and sufficient response equipment are not in place. After months of litigation, the *Balsa 37* pilot, who had a lengthy record of driving an automobile under the influence of alcohol, was deemed responsible for the three-ship collision.

Safely crossing under the bridges of Tampa Bay isn't the only threat a harbor pilot must face. As commerce has grown, the bay has become a network of ninety miles of specific routes connecting nine federally recognized ports. Commercial traffic to and from these Tampa Bay ports must be guided by the trained and experienced hand of a certified harbor pilot. From the southernmost Port Manatee to Port Sutton, Eastbay and Tampa at the northernmost section of the bay, these natural and dredged waterways are today the responsibility of a cadre of twenty-three Tampa Bay pilots who are members of the Florida Harbor Pilots Association. Since 1868, this group of skilled ship drivers has been responsible for the safe and efficient movement of vessels in the state's fourteen deep-water ports, a $50 billion cargo import/export industry that includes transporting more than ten million passengers.

Originally, harbor pilots were stationed at Egmont Key, where the lighthouse water tower made an ideal observation point and approaching ships could be easily spotted, boarded and guided in or out of the harbor. Today, armed with laptops and the most sophisticated weather- and navigation-monitoring equipment available, ship pilots sometimes move their huge vessels to within feet of each other. But one of the most dangerous aspects of their job seems more mundane. The boarding or disembarking of ships in rough seas is a formidable challenge. Several pilots have been killed during this sometimes dangerous rope-ladder transfer.

In November 2012, Captain Carolyn Kurtz, Tampa's first female pilot, received the International Business Person of the Year Award from Tampa Bay's Women in International Trade. A twenty-six-year veteran navigator, Kurtz graduated from the U.S. Merchant Marine Academy in 1986. She immediately joined Maritime Overseas Corp. as a third officer. After earning her unlimited master's license, she went to sea for two years (a qualifying requirement) and in 1995 became the first woman to enter and complete the Florida harbor pilot training program.

Because of its immense size and hectic ship activity, Tampa Bay is almost its own ecosystem; thunderstorms can be drenching one area while balmy sunshine shimmers on bay waters just a few miles away. For that reason, the National Oceanic and Atmospheric Administration's National Weather Service now has three National Weather Service meteorologists specifically assigned to keep ship pilots up to date on all phases of area weather. During a typical five- or six-hour passage through Tampa Bay, the weather can change dramatically. The instant weather advisory system now being tested could have quite possibly averted the collision of the *Summit Venture* had it been available.

POST-SPAN

Eugene C. Figg Jr.
1937–2002

Eugene C. Figg Jr. (1937–2002). *Courtesy of Florida Memory Project.*

"The man who loved bridges" died of leukemia on March 20, 2002, at age sixty-five. His colleagues knew him as an engineer with a passion for creating structurally and aesthetically distinctive bridges. A leading pioneer of segmental concrete and cable-stayed bridge design, his goal was "to build bridges that are functional works of art." Figg's forty-year career established him as the eminent designer of signature bridges and earned him more than 150 national and international design awards. The National Endowment for the Arts has presented its distinguished Presidential Design Award to just five bridges, three of them awarded to the Figg Engineering Group: the Blue Ridge Parkway Viaduct, Grandfather Mountain, North Carolina, 1984; the Bob Graham Sunshine Skyway Bridge, Florida, 1988; and most recently, the Natchez Trace Parkway Arches, Tennessee, 1995.

The American Society of Civil Engineers today offers a $3,000 scholarship in Eugene Figg's name to further the education of aspiring bridge designers. Selection is based on appraisal of the applicant's award justification, stated interest in bridge design and construction, educational plan, academic performance and standing, development potential, leadership capacity and financial need. The selected recipient is also eligible to interview for an internship opportunity with the Figg Engineering Group.

Now in its twelfth year, the Eugene C. Figg Medal for Signature Bridges is an honor intended to keep the bridge lover's concepts and ideals in mind. Figg was a strong proponent of public involvement in both the design and construction phase of bridge building. He enjoyed an enviable reputation for bringing in projects ahead of and under budget—a concept rarely exercised.

CHAPTER 9
GRAHAM'S GOLDEN CABLES

1971

Following the *Summit Venture* collision, the original 1954 Sunshine Skyway Bridge returned to two-way traffic duty, while the Florida Department of Transportation converted the remaining approaches of the downed span into fishing piers. Now, for a few bucks, anglers and sightseers alike could travel halfway over the bay in the comfort of their automobile and enjoy the pier. Sunsets, snook and Spanish mackerel beckoned. Florida, in its amazing ability to promote tourism, was now home to the world's longest fishing pier.

Almost immediately, plans began for a new structure. The decision by city and state officials, guided by the ever-present hand of Governor Bob Graham, was to replace rather than repair. Since the original 1954 span was nearing its shelf life and the damaged span was the youngest, the most practical action was to start over. Graham's vision was that of an entirely new structure spanning the bay, and after seven years of construction and a cost of $250 million, it did.

The new Sunshine Skyway Bridge design has its roots as far back as the early seventeenth century, when, on the pope's behalf, carpenter and architect Faustus Verantius designed the first-ever recorded bridge that used a horizontal base connected by vertical cables—a suspension bridge. These cables were attached to a solid upright support, reducing the need for buttresses or piers. Designers expanded on this concept for their Tampa Bay creation.

Similar to the shoreline staging areas used to build the Gandy Bridge and the first two generations of the Skyway, the newest bridge had a huge fabrication yard about four nautical miles away near Port Manatee. Nearly

A major portion of the concrete pouring took place at this assembly yard on the Manatee County side of the bay.

six hundred of the smaller forty-two-foot-wide segments were cast at the rate of about ten per week.

The larger roadway segments, to be used for the center span, measured up to ninety-five feet in width. This hollow concrete tube construction method had been prevalent in Europe since the end of World War II but was still quite new to America. Workers produced up to four of the larger segments per week. Barges would then transport the puzzle pieces to the bridge site.

Governor Graham announced on January 31, 1981, that the old bridge would be replaced with a concrete cable-stayed bridge. The Figg Engineering Company design that he unveiled was revolutionary. Wind tunnel–tested pillars would bear the load of a cantilever roadbed supported by steel cables. This self-supporting feature allowed the roadbed to be free of piers underneath. Unlike previous designs, which used two lengths of cable supporting each side of the driving platform, this particular cable-stayed suspension bridge would support the roadbed down the center only.

With a 1,200-foot main span, 400 feet wider than the previous bridges, the new bridge offered better maneuverability with nearly 200 feet of headroom. Because the bridge was to become part of Florida's Interstate Highway System, rigid guidelines called for the placement of safety features. To prevent another *Summit Venture* catastrophe, strategically placed man-made islands called "dolphins" were constructed to protect the anchorage points of the new bridge. Nearly two stories tall and 60 feet in diameter, the dolphins are positioned in front of the center piers so that an errant vessel would strike them first, thus protecting the bridge.

Yet one odd and essentially unanswered question remains about the planning and construction activities that took place over the next ten years. As stated, the original single span was unharmed in the *Summit Venture* disaster, and potential debris hazards from the fallen structure and the earlier *Blackthorn* accident had been cleared and put to good use as artificial reefs in deeper Gulf waters. But apparently, no one thought it prudent to erect some sort of guardrail system to offer improved protection of the 1954 span.

Throughout construction and for nearly eighteen months following, harbor pilots had to negotiate a path through both the existing north–south span while navigating around, through and between the construction barges, boats and cranes of the new bridge being erected. In hindsight, it is remarkable that another deadly collision did not occur.

Controversy followed the new Skyway construction. Cracks that had formed during the drying process concerned bankers and bureaucrats alike. Governor Graham quickly created a safety review board that declared the structure safe. Construction continued, but not without problems and non-fatal collisions. In November 1984, a 120-foot barge loaded with steel construction forms for the new cable-supported Skyway Bridge broke from its moorings and battered the remaining first-generation

During the construction of the third-generation Skyway, freighters had to navigate through three tricky-at-times openings.

steel girder bridge. Two-way traffic was halted while tugs labored for a day to remove the half-sunken barge and an inspection of the span was conducted. One of many pleasure craft accidents involved two sailors in 1985 who misjudged the height of their 36-foot sailboat mast. Eckerd College search and rescue crews came to their aid. The bridge and crew were fine; the boat was a mess.

The twenty-one steel tubes on each pylon have already had the high-strength cable ropes pulled through them. The cables were then joined to the deck with hydraulic jacks, and the pipes were filled with a cement grout. It's no wonder students of English get confused—telephone repairmen call their wire cable "lines," bridge builders call their cables "ropes" and seamen call their ropes "lines." Nevertheless, the forty-two steel tube cables were painted with a special-formula paint appropriately named Skyway Yellow.

The cables used to support this massive structure are actually a series of smaller wire "ropes" that have been pulled through steel tubes and cemented in place. The bundle of cable ends was eventually fastened to the concrete deck. The "cables" that are visible from the roadway are actually steel tubes, some as large as nine inches in diameter. Painting the cables about every five years is necessary to prevent salt air corrosion.

Not a job for the faint of heart, workers climb the temporary stairways on either side of the north pylon of the Skyway Bridge.

While it is said that form follows function, the criteria for a bridge must consider length, load, longevity, terrain and available resources. The new Skyway accomplishes the objective of spanning Tampa Bay, and it does so with style and grace. At night, with its brilliant yellow cables lit for all to see, it is more than just a bridge. It is the icon of Florida's west coast, if not the entire state.

A total of forty-eight main support piers were specified in the Sunshine Skyway contract, with the largest two structures bordering the main 1,200-foot-wide bridge opening. The elliptical shape of the high piers was intended to reduce drag in hurricane-force winds. Concrete bridge sections were precast offsite at the Port of Manatee casting yard and then brought by barge to the site, where they were stacked, bolted together and weighed. Some weighed as much as fifty-four tons.

Another bridge collision involving the "new" third-generation bridge was simply unacceptable to engineers, who then developed a system of protective

Left: These concrete open-box structures were reinforced with cross members that also served as connection points for the overhead support cables.

Below: In this overhead view, dozens of workers look almost like ants as the last 220-ton precast concrete section is eased into the opening between the ends of the bridge. Note the American flag (lower left corner) flying proudly as the notable August 23, 1986, event unfolded. *Courtesy of* St. Petersburg Times.

bumpers called "dolphins." The largest of these safety devices, at the base of the main span, can withstand almost 30 million pounds of force. They cost nearly $4 million, but considering they protect a $250 million bridge, they were a wise investment. As the hydraulic lifts closed the final gap, bringing the final sections together, it's easy to imagine a foreman shouting, "Watch your hands—watch your fingers!" The precision lift, completed in just over two hours, was cause for celebration. Thrill-seeking pleasure boaters watched from near the main passage.

Soaring nineteen stories over the salt-laced waters of Tampa Bay, the Sunshine Skyway Bridge is large enough to accommodate the Port of Tampa, one of the nation's busiest seaports. With more than a dozen design awards, including recognition by the National Endowment for the Arts, the bridge is an icon of the Tampa Bay area and the "flag bridge" of Florida. Considered one of the most recognized bridges in the United States, it was rated among the "World's Top 10 Bridges" by the Travel Channel.

In 1954, O'Neil's Marina entered into an agreement with the City of St. Petersburg to build and operate a facility at the southern tip of the city.

The three generations of the Sunshine Skyway Bridge.

The flagship bridge of Florida, the Bob Graham Sunshine Skyway Bridge. *Courtesy of* St. Petersburg Times.

Profits from the facility were shared with the city, but highway officials originally threatened to take over the area for a new bridge approach. Ultimately, compromises were made, and a redesigned marina continued a long tradition of servicing local boaters and fishermen.

World War II navy veteran Jack Thomas thought his fighting days were over when he opened Skyway Jack's Restaurant at the south end of the peninsula. Along with O'Neill's Marina, it was a favorite Pinellas Point hangout for fishermen and tourists. When planners said the new bridge required more land and that he'd have to move, Jack disagreed. He fought with Tallahassee but lost the argument. The popular eatery relocated to its present Thirty-fourth Street South location.

After the new Skyway Bridge was finished, the old structure was demolished, but not before Wes MacIntire and his wife were permitted to drive over it. The couple stopped at the top to drop thirty-five white carnations into the water, one for each victim of the May 9, 1980, *Summit Venture* disaster. They were the last of the general public to cross the old bridge.

Florida state senator Bob Graham campaigned for governor with a "workday" program where he took on the jobs of everyday people, from housewife to policeman to short-order cook. Once elected, he retained his supporters by continuing the workday idea. As governor, Graham fought for construction of the present-day Skyway Bridge, spending a hard-hat workday there as well.

As part of the ceremonies formally opening the bridge, organizers staged a marathon, promoted as "20,000 Feet Over the Sea." The event drew almost fifteen thousand runners, so really they could have claimed 30,000 feet. Marathon record holder Bill Rodgers led a three-mile run from the north end of the bridge, while Boston Marathoner Joan Benoit Samuelson headed a second three-miler from the Manatee side. They met in the center and boarded buses for a return ride to their respective starting areas. Two other 10K races started at opposite ends and went entirely across the 195-foot-high span. The twelve-dollar entry fees raised money for the Leukemia Society. The graceful third-generation or "new" bridge seems to dwarf its predecessors, but the approach spans leading up to the 1,200-foot main span have only a 4 percent slope, which allows for good traffic flow.

A full-page ad promoting the opening of the first Skyway Bridge boasted that nearly three-quarters of a million bags of Portland cement were used in the 1954 project. That number, of course, pales in comparison to the hollow concrete method used with the third-generation bridge and its 200,000 cubic yards of cement. The wire "rope" used to make the cable supports would reach from St. Petersburg to Atlanta.

In the mid-1980s, designers made glowing predictions that the cable-strung beauty across the bay would last up to one hundred years. But that may be optimistic. The bridge is continuously monitored and inspected, but as early as 1995, cracks in the main span foundations had been detected. Potential problems detected in the new bridge included deteriorating Teflon bearings that allow the bridge to "breathe" and keep parts from binding. Some protective seals around the steel cable tubes were also found to be deteriorating. Still, the structure was—and is today—considered by engineers to be safe. State engineers said the bearing wear was expected and was not alarming.

After seven long years, nearly 200,000 cubic yards of concrete and 447 miles of cable strands were merged to create an awe-inspiring monument to man, machine and Mother Nature. Bob Graham, who himself labored on the structure as a steel worker during one of his famous campaign "workdays," called the Skyway "a tribute to dreams of the human mind and skill of the worker's hands."

The task of destroying the damaged Skyway Bridge went to George Brown, a Tampa Bay native with an international reputation as the go-to guy for blowing things up. By 1992, he had already exploded 440 bridges in the southeastern United States, including the original Gandy Bridge. Working alone, the Sunshine Skyway project was the largest demolition of "Boom-Boom Brown's" career and, at the time, the largest demolition project in the world.

Just months after its completion, the original Skyway Bridge was saddled with a new media identity and a macabre group of followers fascinated with bridge-jumping suicides. Since 1956, the number of attempted suicide jumps from the Sunshine Skyway Bridge varies, ranging from a low of 130 to a claimed high of 206. Today, followers of these frequently misunderstood deaths list the Sunshine Skyway Bridge as the third most fatal bridge in America. San Francisco's Golden Gate Bridge has the dubious distinction of hosting the most suicide jumps annually. Statistics indicate, however, that firearms for men and poison for women are the two top methods chosen by those intent on ending their own lives.

According to data compiled by the Violence Prevention Division of the Center for Disease Control, suicide was the eleventh leading cause of death for all ages in this country in 2007. More than thirty-four thousand suicides occurred that year, the equivalent of ninety-four per day. Without downplaying the seriousness of suicide of any type, most emergency responders agree that a bridge jump is a dreadful and probably agonizing way to end one's life. From the crest of the bridge, it only takes about 3.5 seconds for a body to drop about 190 feet, slamming into the water at seventy-five miles per hour, shattering limbs and exploding internal organs but not instantly killing a person. Most are so badly injured and immobilized that they die by drowning.

In 1999, Skyway became the first bridge in the nation to install solar-powered Crisis Center telephones along the bridge, connecting callers directly to a trained suicide intervention contact. The Sunshine Skyway and numerous other long bridges throughout the country have for many years had emergency phone boxes strategically located along their length, but they were linked to highway patrol dispatchers or bridge operators for the purpose of reporting traffic problems.

According to Carol A. Toffolon, director of marketing and public relations at the Crisis Center of Tampa Bay, the center received seventeen calls on the bridge phone line over the latest twelve-month period, which ended September 30, 2012. Not counting routine test calls, thirteen of these calls were stranded motorists, to whom assistance was dispatched. Two calls were silent calls, for which an intervention agent was sent to investigate. One call came from a witness to a jumper, while another came from a suicidal caller—intervention agents were sent in both instances. Critics of the red box Crisis Center phones claimed they were "too little, too late," as a suicidal individual who had made it to the top of a span was difficult to stop.

But, if a good side can be found in the whole subject of bridge jumpers and suicide, it is this: mental health professionals have been able to use these unfortunate deaths as illustrations for education and prevention. Organizations like the Jason Foundation, which centers on teen suicide; the U.S. Department of Health; the National Institute for Mental Health; and the National Suicide Prevention Hotline (1-800-273-TALK) have all made great advances in educating the public in finding ways to treat and reduce this disturbing problem. The Crisis Center of Tampa Bay (dial 2-1-1) not only provides suicide prevention and support for at-risk individuals and their families but also offers free crisis counseling and referral to over 4,600 community resources twenty-four hours a day, 365 days a year.

The American Bridge Company served as general contractor on the Sunshine Skyway Bridge in a joint venture with Paschen Construction and the Morrison Knudsen Company. Other notable American Bridge structures include the San Francisco–Oakland Bay Bridge, Oakland, California, 1936; the Mackinac Bridge, Mackinac Straits, Michigan, 1957; and New York Harbor's Verrazano-Narrows Bridge, finished in 1964.

Using "bridge-speak," the American Bridge Co. described the current Sunshine Skyway Bridge as an 8,858-foot structure consisting of three major parts. The dramatic center portion is the 2,280- by 85-foot-wide precast segmental cable-stayed main bridge with a 1,200-foot main span erected by the balanced cantilever method. That's a mouthful, so most people just say, "It's beautiful."

In November 2005, Florida Department of Transportation bridge #150189 was rededicated to carry its champion's name: the Bob Graham Sunshine Skyway Bridge. The inventory number remained unchanged. In a dedication-day speech, Senator Graham said:

> *Our current achievement that shines brightly over the waters, spanning the currents below, remains a proud gateway to Tampa Bay. This functional work of art not only offers a ten-minute commuter connection with a spectacular panoramic view, it speaks to what can be accomplished. The Sunshine Skyway allows us to reach further. It challenges us to dream bigger dreams.*

POST-SPAN

Daniel Robert "Bob" Graham
1936–

At first glance, if one were to review a *complete* resume of Daniel Robert Graham, his reaction would have to be, "This guy can't hold a job!"

In 1977, during his early political life as a state senator, Bob Graham happened upon a campaign gimmick that made him a household name. Responding to a challenge from a frustrated schoolteacher, Graham announced he would experience the lives of ordinary Floridians firsthand by working their jobs. Thus, teaching Sue Reilly's Carol City High School class became the first of more than 921 different jobs Graham would perform throughout his political life.

The idea of getting closer to everyday people and their experiences was not completely new; Lawton Chiles had proved that by walking across

Zookeeper Bob Graham tends to a rhino during one of his workday jobs. *Courtesy of* St. Petersburg Times.

Florida to win his 1970 U.S. Senate seat. Former Tennessee governor Lamar Alexander, in his trademark plaid shirt, would trek his Volunteer State in the same way. But Bob Graham's workday program sparked an interest and trust from the men and women on the street—Florida's "normal working folks." To make the idea legitimate, the press was allowed only limited access to the workday job. Graham performed all aspects of the job, if at all possible, and worked an entire shift. He spent one of those trademark workdays as a riveter on the iconic bridge that, in 2005, would be officially renamed the Bob Graham Sunshine Skyway Bridge, in honor of his efforts to move it from the drawing board to reality in a remarkably short six years.

The thirty-eighth governor of Florida (1979–87) and U.S. Senator (1987–2005) has now added author to his legendary list of workday jobs. In 2011, Graham published his first novel, the thriller *The Keys to the Kingdom*, which was selected as a Bronze medal recipient in 2011 by the Florida Humanities Council.

Graham, a former shrimper, short-order cook, bellhop, social worker, plumber and housewife (just to name a few), is now concentrating his efforts on the newly established Bob Graham Center for Public Service at his undergraduate alma mater, the University of Florida. He also serves as chairman of the Commission on the Prevention of Weapons of Mass Destruction Proliferation and Terrorism.

INTO THE NEXT CENTURY

An official September 2010 state inspection of the Sunshine Skyway earned the bridge a "health index" rating of 86.83. The Florida Department of Transportation uses this 100-point scale as a tool to measure the overall condition of bridges. Typically, the index includes about a dozen different elements that are evaluated by the department. A health index below 85 generally indicates that some repairs are needed, although it doesn't mean the bridge is unsafe. A lower health index means that more work is probably required to improve the bridge to an ideal condition. Among other items, officials are looking at worn-out Teflon bearing pads, corrosion, paint condition and evidence of some concrete erosion.

Safety has always been of paramount importance to highway, port and other regulatory agencies throughout the state. They regularly implement new ways to deter suicide attempts, monitor and control traffic flow and, most recently, to protect all public waterways and bridges from the threat of terrorism. Routine underwater inspections by trained divers are an important part of the department's safety inspection program. FDOT officials provide ample public information and are eager to discuss most state projects, but in the interest of national security, structural details, blueprints and certain testing data are now provided on a strict need-to-know basis.

In a June 2012 surprise move, Hillsborough County commissioners unanimously agreed to delay demolition of the 1956 version of the Gandy Bridge. Known as the Friendship Trail Bridge, the structure, still adorned with its 1950s-era streetlights, was a favorite walking, jogging and biking route for thousands of residents on both sides of the bay. By 2008, safety had become an issue, and engineers closed the structure to all, claiming the bridge was so dangerously deteriorated that it could collapse under its own weight. The new reprieve is intended to give the public an opportunity to tell commissioners what they want and what they are willing to pay for. The measure could be decided at the ballot box.

The Port of Tampa, with a channel depth of forty-three feet, is the largest tonnage facility of Florida's twelve ports and one of the busiest in the nation. But bigger isn't always better, at least not when it comes to navigating under the Sunshine Skyway Bridge. There are at least two megaliners (with others reportedly on the drawing board) that are too big to enter Tampa Bay. But neither the local cruise line industry nor local officials seem to view this as much of a serious loss of business. The estuary known as Tampa Bay has been traversed by bridge and by boat, and recently there's been one interesting but unlikely suggestion of a light rail connection.

The Sunshine Skyway Bridge is a golden doorway to and from this port facility that generates billions of dollars annually in trade to virtually every corner of the world. Hopefully, huge technological advancements in weather tracking and navigation will forever prevent another bridge collision disaster.

Over the years, virtually all of the bridges crossing Tampa Bay have at one time or another been sideswiped, rammed or bumped by both commercial and private vessels. Unlike the Sunshine Skyway Bridge, these accidents fortunately have not claimed lives, but property has been damaged and in some cases vessels have been lost. Authorities can only estimate the number of private boating mishaps and near misses that have occurred along sections of the Campbell Causeway, the Frankland and Gandy Bridges and the Skyway. It's believed that a majority of these incidents go unreported. However, routine inspections of bay bridges, piers and pilings help detect possible structural damage like chipped or cracked concrete and rotted pilings. Frequently, the Coast Guard or commercial towing services are called to recover or assist a boat that has been involved in an accident. Because of licensing, harbor pilot regulations and other operational restrictions, authorities do maintain records of mishaps involving commercial barges and ships.

On February 28, 2012, the U.S. Postal Service recognized the twenty-fifth anniversary of Florida's Sunshine Skyway Bridge by issuing the $5.15 Sunshine Skyway Bridge Priority Mail stamp. The stamp, designed by Carl T. Hermann of Nevada, showcases a digital illustration created by artist Dan Cosgrove of Chicago. Speakers at the ceremony included former Florida governor Charlie Crist, who praised the span's functionality and its aesthetic appeal.

U.S. Postal Service district manager Nancy Rettinghouse (left) assists former governor Charlie Crist in unveiling the new Sunshine Skyway postage stamp. *Courtesy of Robert Neff, Fifth World Art.*

Assisting in the stamp unveiling was the newly appointed U.S. Postal Service district manager Nancy Rettinghouse, who called the span "a modern masterpiece," noting that it shared a common goal with the postal service: "They connect people."

Crist, who grew up in St. Petersburg, recalled how "the signature of Tampa Bay" was born out of the horrific. "What was a tragedy became a beautiful thing," he said.

Also on hand was Michael Cegelis, senior vice-president of the American Bridge Company, who stressed how a demanding construction schedule was met: "Seven years for a new bridge…it's remarkable to get a bridge conceived, built and delivered in that time." Unable to attend, former Florida governor Bob Graham said in a prepared statement, "The new bridge memorialized the thirty-five people who lost their lives in the *Summit Venture* collapse…[and] unified the communities of Tampa Bay."

As recently as June 25, 2012, all or portions of all four spans across the bay were closed to automobile traffic. Tropical storm Debbie had made her way north through the Gulf of Mexico and brought up to twelve inches of rain and fifty-mile-per-hour winds to large sections of Florida's west coast. Those swirling winds, though not presenting a threat to the bridge itself, prompted authorities to halt Sunshine Skyway traffic for almost forty-eight hours. It was the longest continuous closing to motor vehicle traffic in the bridge's history. Flooded curbs and standing water also forced the temporary closing of northbound lanes on the W. Howard Frankland Bridge, and both the Gandy Bridge and Courtney Campbell Causeway stopped traffic for short intervals as wind-whipped waters washed across the barely above-sea-level pavement. The fact remains that spanning the bay is ultimately up to Mother Nature.

Post-Span

Kenneth M. King aka "Sky King"
1944–

Ken King grew up in Century, Florida, a panhandle sawmill town where almost everybody lived in a company house and owed the company store. It was a tightknit community where neighbors knew one another, and if you were a kid up to no good, your parents knew about it before you got home. Ken's family and the community stressed honesty, respect and hard work. The U.S. Marine Corps reinforced those values. "When I was a kid, I saw John Wayne in *The Sands of Iowa Jima*," King recalled, "and I knew right then I wanted to be a marine."

A meritorious Non-Commissioned Officer (NCO) advancement program sent King to Officer Candidate School and then to Vietnam, where on at least two occasions, the man in front of him was instantly killed by an exploding mine. His service awards included a Purple Heart and Bronze Star. Upon discharge, he married his wife, Lee, settled down in Bradenton, joined the Florida Highway Patrol (FHP) and enrolled in night school to earn his degree. "I'd get out of class, get into my uniform and start my shift about midnight," he recalled. It was a busy schedule, and one that put the six-foot-one 210-pounder on the Sunshine Skyway Bridge almost every night—in a position to save the lives of at least ten would-be suicide jumpers. By the time he had thwarted his third suicide, the *Bradenton Herald* had dubbed him "Sky King," a play on TV's popular crime-fighting, Cessna-flying rancher.

When faced with a jumper, King said it was a matter of listening, agreeing, cajoling and, if necessary, a little wrestling:

> *I had one big guy who had already climbed over the railing and was ready to go. I grabbed him, hanging on for dear life. He was really big, and he almost got the best of me. I had no interest in going over the side with him. I finally managed to handcuff him to the rail.*

By the time help arrived, the jumper had calmed down.

"Adapt, modify, overcome," is a phrase marines commonly recite when facing a tough mission, but King chuckles when talking about one of his creative solutions. A jumper who had climbed up into the bridge superstructure refused to budge unless he could have a drink. "It just so happened," King recalled, "that I had a half-pint of confiscated whiskey in my patrol car. He made me step back from the bottle, climbed down, chugged it in one long swig and said, 'OK, let's go.'"

In 1974, Sky King was chosen from among 1,100 FHP officers as "Trooper of the Year." He downplays this achievement, but there's a hint of pride in his voice as he recalls receiving a congratulatory note from Kirby Grant, the actor who portrayed the "real" Sky King on television.

Kenneth King aka "Sky King" shares a proud moment with his wife, Lee, after being selected as "Florida Trooper of the Year" in 1974. *Courtesy of Kenneth King.*

Two years later, the father of two resigned from the FHP and moved his family to Washington, D.C., so he could work for the U.S. Bureau of Alcohol, Tobacco and Firearms (ATF). He was assigned to the New Orleans office. Then, in 1993, he led a ten-man ATF special response team to Waco, Texas, to arrest David Koresh and his Branch Davidian followers for possession of illegal fully automatic weapons. The ensuing mêlée, seen on live TV, resulted in the death of four federal agents, three from King's own team. He survived six bullet wounds in his back, stomach, chest and both arms, but his law enforcement career was over. He and Lee retired to Tennessee's Smoky Mountains.

To have survived Waco, Vietnam and the Sunshine Skyway Bridge, the now-widowed King agrees he certainly has a guardian angel. And like most who once wore the uniform, he proudly proclaims he's not a *former* marine, he's just "temporarily unassigned." Semper Fi, Sky King, Semper Fi.

SELECTED BIBLIOGRAPHY

Arsenault, Raymond. *St. Petersburg and the Florida Dream, 1888–1950*. Norfolk, VA: Donning Co., 1988.

Ayers, R. Wayne. *St. Petersburg: The Sunshine City*. Charleston, SC: Arcadia Publishing, 2001.

Baker, Rick. *Mangroves to Major League: A Timeline of St. Petersburg, Florida*. St. Petersburg, FL: Southern Heritage Press, 2000.

Bill, Ledyard. *A Winter in Florida*. New York: Wood & Holdbrook, 1869.

Billington, David P. *The Tower and the Bridge*. New York: Basic Books Inc., 1983.

Bothwell, Dick. "Sunshine 200." *St. Petersburg Times*, 1949.

"C. of C. Plans Drive to Bring War Workers Here." *St. Petersburg Times*, June 29, 1943.

"City Now Large Enough to Have Both Tourists and Industries." *St. Petersburg Times*, December 24, 1941.

"City Plans Ads in 44 Papers, 12 Magazines." *St. Petersburg Times*, September 9, 1943.

Dahlem, Ted. "Interview with Huddy "Buck" LeVar of the Bee Line Ferry." April 16, 1998. Federal Writer's Project, Courtesy of the St. Petersburg Museum of History.

"Eastern Air Transport." *Wall Street Journal*, December 19, 1930.

Federal Writers' Project. *Florida: A Guide to the Southernmost State*. New York: Oxford University Press, 1939.

"$50,000 Ad Fund for City Urged." *St. Petersburg Times*, June 22, 1943.

"Florida Construction." *Wall Street Journal*, January 9, 1926.

"Florida Real Estate Sales." *Wall Street Journal*, April 1, 1930.

"For Many, Sunshine Skyway Bridge Is a Dark Symbol of Sadness and Loss." *St. Petersburg Times*, April 13, 1998.

"Frankland Bridge Dedication Begins Progress Era." *Evening Independent*, January 15, 1960.

"Frankland Bridge Opens to Traffic." *St. Petersburg Times*, January 16, 1960.

Frazer, William, and John Guthrie Jr. *The Florida Land Boom: Speculation, Money and the Banks*. Westport, CT: Greenwood Publishing, 1995.

Fuller, Walter P. *St. Petersburg and Its People*. St. Petersburg, FL: Great Outdoors Publishing, 1972.

"Gandy Bridge." *Wall Street Journal*, January 14, 1926.

Gannon, Michael, ed. "World War II" in *The New History of Florida*. Gainesville: University Press of Florida, 1996.

"Governor Collins Officially Opens New Bay Bridge." *Evening Independent*, January 15, 1960.

Grismer, Karl. *The History of St. Petersburg*. N.p.: Tourist News Publishing, 1924.

————. *The Story of St. Petersburg: The History of Lower Pinellas Peninsula and the Sunshine City*. N.p.: P.K. Smith and Co., 1948.

"Helped Build Better City, Mayor States." *St. Petersburg Times*, October 17, 1942.

"Here is Your Place in the Sun." *New York Times*, December 2, 1934.

Hooker, Robert. "The Times and Its Times." St. Petersburg, FL: The Times Publishing Co., 1984.

Hurley, Frank T., Jr. *Surf, Sand and Postcard Sunsets: A History of Pass-A Grille and the Gulf Beaches*. St. Petersburg, FL: Great Outdoors Publishing, 1977.

"I'll See You in Sunny St. Petersburg." *New York Times*, December 10, 1933.

Jackson, Page S. *St. Petersburg: An Informal History*. St. Petersburg, FL: Great Outdoors Publishing, 1962.

"John Lodwick." *New York Times*, October 17, 1942.

Leader, Hernando. "Alfred A. McKethan Dies." *St. Petersburg Times*, April 2, 2002.

Matus, Ron. "Old Salt Spreads His Love of the Harmonica." *St. Petersburg Times*, June 28, 2002.

"The Men Who Bridged the Bay." *St. Petersburg Times*, July 14, 1980.

Miller, Betty Jean. "'Pop' Gandy Had Vision of a Bridge." *St. Petersburg Times*, November 23, 1987.

"More Florida Tourists." *Wall Street Journal*, May 20, 1933.

Morgan, Philip. "An Amazing Span." *Tampa Tribune*, September 6, 2004, final edition, sec. B2.

Mormino, Gary. *Hillsborough Goes to War: The Home Front, 1940–1950*. Tampa, FL: Tampa Bay History Center, 2001.

Mullins, Miriam. "The Day the War Ended: A Remembrance." *St. Petersburg Times*, July 25, 1995.

Pinellas Planning Council. "Historical Background of Pinellas County, Florida: Technical Report No. 3." 1968.

Powers, Walter. "One of World's Most Unusual Bridges Steadily Rising in Lower Tampa Bay." *Tampa Tribune*, January 2, 1953.

Richter, Linda K. "State-Sponsored Tourism." *Public Administration Review* 45, no. 6 (November–December 1985): 832–39.

Sitler, Nevin D. *Selling St. Petersburg: John Lodwick and the Promotion of a Florida Paradise*. St. Petersburg, FL, 2006.

"Southland's First Airship Base Located at St. Petersburg." *Cedar Rapids Tribune*, December 28, 1928.

"St. Petersburg Awaiting Half Million Guests." *Chicago Daily Tribune*, December 11, 1938.

St. Petersburg Board of Trade. Promotional Pamphlet. St. Petersburg, FL: St. Petersburg Museum of History, Chamber of Commerce Collections, 1919.

St. Petersburg Chamber of Commerce. *Sunshine Skyway Commemorative Book*. St. Petersburg, FL, 1954.

"St. Petersburg Claims State Tourist Crown." *Florida Times-Union*, May 7, 1946.

Stinemetz, Morgan. "The Bee Line Ferry Was a Great Way to Travel." *Sarasota Herald Tribune*, October 11, 2004, Manatee Edition, sec. B4.

Stockbridge, Frank P., and John H. Perry. *Florida in the Making*. New York: De Bower Publishing Co., 1926.

Taylor, Scott. "Ferryman Logged 52,300 Trips Before Bridge Arrived." *St. Petersburg Times*, February 2, 2000.

"This Was Florida's Boom." St. Petersburg, FL: The Times Publishing Co., 1954.

"Tourism: A Good Value for Pinellas County." *Suncoast Magazine* (October–November 1985).

Van Bibber, W.C. "Peninsular and Sub-Peninsular Air and Climates." *Journal of the American Medical Association* 4 (1885).

Waggoner, Holly. *Skyway to the Sun*. Sarasota, FL: Omnigraphis Publishers, 1988.

Weiss, Thomas. "Tourism in America Before World War II." *Journal of Economic History* 64, no. 2 (2004).

Wickman, John E. "Ike and 'The Great Truck Train'—1919." *Kansas History* 13, no. 3 (August 1990).

Witwer, Stan. "A Great Bridge Starts across the Lower Bay." *St. Petersburg Times*, May 3, 1953.

INDEX